AIR VANGUARD 10

GENERAL DYNAMICS F-111 AARDVARK

PETER DAVIES

First published in Great Britain in 2013 by Osprey Publishing:
PO Box 883, Oxford, OX1 9PL, UK
PO Box 3985, New York, NY 10185-3985, USA
E-mail: info@ospreypublishing.com

Osprey Publishing is part of the Osprey Group

A CIP catalogue record for this book is available from the
British Library

Print ISBN: 978 1 78096 611 3
PDF ebook ISBN: 978 1 78096 612 0
ePub ebook ISBN: 978 1 78096 613 7

Index by Zoe Ross
Typeset in Deca Sans and Sabon
Originated by PDQ Media, Bungay, UK
Printed in China through Asia Pacific Offset Limited

13 14 15 16 17 10 9 8 7 6 5 4 3 2 1

Osprey Publishing is supporting the Woodland Trust, the UK's leading
woodland conservation charity, by funding the dedication of trees.

www.ospreypublishing.com

ACKNOWLEDGEMENTS

I am most grateful to all those who assisted with this book. Among
them were the following retired USAF personnel:

Lt Col Steve Altick, Lt Col Willliam Baker, Col Ron Barker, Col Bob
Brotzman, Capt Craig Brown, Maj Richard Brown, Lt Col Jack Funke, Col
Tom Germscheid, MSgt Steven R. Hyre, Maj Jim Icenhour, Capt Brad
Insley, Col Bob Pahl, Col Larry Peters, Lt Col Edwin Wells; with particular
thanks to Maj Jim 'Mr Vark' Rotramel.

GLOSSARY

AAA	Anti-Aircraft Artillery
AB	Air Base
AF	Air Force
AFB	Air Force Base
AGM	Air-to-Ground Missile
AIR	Air Inflatable Retard
AMARC	Aerospace Maintenance and Regeneration Center
AMP	Avionics Modernization Program
AoA	Angle of Attack
ARS	Attack Radar System
AUP	Avionics Update Program
BLU	Bomb Live Unit
BuNo	Bureau of Aeronautics Number (US Navy)
CADC	Central Air Data Computer
CBU	Cluster Bomb Unit
CCTS	Combat Crew Training Squadron
ECM	Electronic Counter-Measures
ECS	Electronic Combat Squadron (USAF)
FLIR	Forward-Looking Infrared
FS	Fighter Squadron
GBU	Guided Bomb Unit
GD	General Dynamics Corporation
HARM	High-speed Anti-Radiation Missile
IFF	Identification, Friend or Foe
INS	Inertial Navigation System
LCOS	Lead-Computing Optical Sight
LDGP	Low-Drag General Purpose (bomb)
LGB	Laser-Guided Bomb
LLLGB	Low-Level Laser-Guided Bomb
MFD	Multi-Function Display
NASA	National Aeronautics and Space Administration
PAVE	Precision Avionics Vectoring Equipment
RAAF	Royal Australian Air Force
SAC	Strategic Air Command (USAF)
SAM	Surface-to-Air Missile
SRAM	Short-Range Attack Missile (Boeing AGM-69A)
SUU	Suspension Underwing Unit
TAC	Tactical Air Command (USAF)
TACAN	Tactical Aid to Navigation
TACT	Transonic Aircraft Technology
TFR	Terrain-Following Radar
TFS	Tactical Fighter Squadron (USAF)
TFTS	Tactical Fighter Training Squadron (USAF)
TFW	Tactical Fighter Wing (USAF)
USAFE	United States Air Forces in Europe
WCTB	Wing Carry-Through Box
WSO	Weapons System Officer

CONTENTS

GENERAL DYNAMICS F-111 AARDVARK

INTRODUCTION

The F-111's reputation as one of the most underestimated and misunderstood 20th-century combat aircraft can be traced to its designation. 'F-111', indicating a fighter type, never fitted a 75ft-long aircraft sometimes weighing up to 100,000lb. Although the US Navy might have made a credible bomber-destroying missile platform from their short-lived F-111B version, operational land-based F-111s sometimes carried only a token air-to-air missile (AAM) or cannon for self-defence. Rather than air-to-air combat, tactics called for a low-altitude, high-speed run to safety, and F-111s never flew the air-superiority missions that were first written into the design. However, the aircraft's performance as a long-range strike and interdiction bomber from 1967 until its retirement over 40 years later was so outstanding that many believed it still had irreplaceable qualities in 2010.

Its original designation, 'TFX' (Tactical Fighter, Experimental) was a better guide to its true purpose. It was meant to replace the Republic F-105 Thunderchief, another fighter used almost exclusively for bombing. In addition, the US Air Force (USAF) wanted a similar aircraft to the US Navy's Grumman A-6 Intruder, with its sophisticated all-weather, single-aircraft attack capability. Sadly, inter-service and political tensions all contributed to the F-111's persistently negative early reception. The USAF's 1958 General Operational Requirement for a new tactical fighter had optimistically specified Mach 2+, a 60,000ft ceiling and vertical or short take-off, modified in 1960 to require 3,000ft 'rough field' take-offs and landings. At the same time the US Navy required a long-endurance fleet-defence interceptor able to carry numerous long-range AAMs in an extended subsonic orbit.

President John F. Kennedy's business-trained Secretary of Defense, Robert S. McNamara, renowned for his organizational and cost-saving strategies, was tasked with bringing greater efficiency to the US forces and defence industry. He initiated designs with 'commonality' to meet the needs of both services, which he felt had too many different aircraft types. He also saw TFX as a replacement for many Strategic Air Command (SAC) bombers, but also able to meet the new USAF requirement for 'flexible response' with conventional, non-nuclear ordnance.

As design negotiations proceeded on what a later congressional investigation called 'the largest single airplane contract that has ever been awarded' (with an estimated production run of 3,000 aircraft), military chiefs became increasingly discontented, feeling that McNamara was forcing them to accept an unworkable compromise for purely financial reasons. It also became clear to the General Dynamics (GD) designers at Fort Worth in Texas that the USAF F-111A version would weigh almost double their original 37,000lb estimate, to which Gen Frank F. Everest, head of Tactical Air Command (TAC), responded curtly, 'I'm not going to accept any goddamned 70,000lb airplane'. Early F-111As actually weighed over 91,000lb fully loaded, and massive weight inflation contributed to the cancellation of the naval F-111B in 1968.

As the pioneer of many innovations, the F-111A faced development problems that required time-consuming tests and modifications. For optimum performance

Bell's two X-5 prototypes (50-1838 and 50-1839) began to test variable-sweep wings on 20 June 1951 at Edwards AFB, using the roller-and-rail wing 'translation' mechanism for the first time on 27 July. (USAF)

throughout the speed range it introduced and proved the variable-sweep wing, adopted in subsequent aircraft such as the Grumman F-14 Tomcat, Rockwell B-1 Lancer, Panavia Tornado, Tupolev Tu-22, Mikoyan-Gurevich MiG-23 and Sukhoi Su-24. F-111s were powered by the world's first afterburning turbofan with supersonic performance. This concept too would become generally accepted, but in the F-111 the process of matching the engines to their innovative variable-spike air inlets caused delays that played into its critics' hands.

For the USAF's 'under-the-radar', all-weather attack missions, usually flown in darkness, the F-111 required complex terrain-following radar (TFR) and inertial navigation/attack systems that could fly the aircraft to its target automatically at 200ft minimum altitude. Although this new system was the key to much of the F-111's capability, it resulted in inevitable teething difficulties and losses that grabbed the headlines in an increasingly hostile US press. Other innovations, such as the US Navy-prescribed crew escape module, replacing conventional ejection seats, were limited to the F-111; but its integrated radar homing and warning (RHAW) suite was another 'first', subsequently adapted for many other tactical aircraft.

With such an unpromising start, it fell to the F-111's crews and developers to prove its true worth as one of the most important aircraft in the Vietnam War, Operation *El Dorado Canyon* and Operation *Desert Storm*; while for Australia, its only export customer, the F-111 was the principal strike aircraft of the Royal Australian Air Force (RAAF) for 37 years.

DESIGN AND DEVELOPMENT

The F-111's best-known characteristic, its variable-sweep wing, originated from the earliest days of jet-powered flight as a way of combining the high-speed advantages of a swept or delta wing with the low-speed handling of a straighter wing. Messerschmitt's supersonic projects designers in Germany in 1943 used pioneering swept-wing research by Adolf Busemann and Albert Betz, including pivoting wings that extended to reduce speed for take-off and landing, particularly from short or damaged runways. Swept back, the same wing could offer the reduced span and low drag needed for high speeds at lower altitudes. Messerschmitt's incomplete P.1101 V1 experimental prototype was shipped to the USA in 1945 and developed by the Bell Aircraft Corporation as the X-5. In flight tests from 1951, however, the X-5's poor handling (particularly a tendency to spin at low speeds) highlighted the severe difficulties in devising suitable variable-sweep aerodynamics. The shift in wing position caused major trimming difficulties as the wing's aerodynamic centre of pressure moved fore and aft during wing sweep. It was thought that the wing root had to be moved forward mechanically as the tip swept back, keeping the wing's aerodynamic centre in line with the aircraft's centre of gravity. This required heavy mechanisms involving rails and rollers that negated the weight advantages of the swing-wing compared with alternative ways of achieving short take-off, such as vertical take-off requiring massive, powerful engines. At the conclusion of testing in 1955 the X-5 project's sponsors, the USAF, saw little point in further investment, although some of the principles of swing-wing technology had been demonstrated.

Parallel US Navy research produced the Grumman XF10F Jaguar in 1952. Based on data obtained from the Bell X-5 flight-test programme, this jet also proved to be unstable. Its sliding wing-root position was complex and the wing became increasingly ineffective as sweep angle increased. Underpowered by the disappointing Westinghouse J40 turbojet, the Jaguar never achieved satisfactory performance levels, although 82 were on order when it was cancelled. However, the sole XF10F-1 yielded valuable data that Grumman used when the company was awarded the US Navy's share of the F-111 development contract.

Swinging wings were also of interest to British designers in the immediate post-war years. At Vickers (Weybridge), Barnes Wallis's 'Wild Goose' supersonic military jet and 'Swallow' intercontinental airliner concepts used laminar flow, variable-geometry wings with flight control provided by pivoting engines, pod-mounted on the wings. Having received no sustained interest from the British government in the mid-1950s, the Vickers team took the idea to NASA's Langley Laboratory in the USA where, as Wallis noted, 'We convinced the Americans too sincerely that this was a great idea and so they decided to take it up for themselves' (rather than funding further British research).

At NASA, aerodynamicist John Stack was impressed by Vickers' decision to extend their design's fuselage outwards in the form of a fixed 'glove', within which the outer wing pivots were located further from the fuselage centreline than on the earlier designs, thus alleviating aerodynamic centre problems. Stack developed the idea around the prospect of a multi-role tactical fighter-bomber, but he also envisaged naval applications. With support from Gen Frank Everest, head of TAC, Stack outlined a variable-geometry aircraft with advanced turbofan engines (another British innovation) for long-range fuel economy. It had advanced avionics and carried up to 30,000lb of ordnance

at sustained supersonic speed over an 800-mile low-level combat radius (400 miles of this at Mach 1.2) from short or unprepared airfields. For rapid deployments it needed a 3,300-mile range to cross the Atlantic unrefuelled, or the Pacific with one in-flight refuelling. In June 1960 the USAF refined these proposals into Specific Operational Requirement (SOR) 183, with a reduced 200-mile dash at Mach 1.2.

Grumman's XF10F-1 Jaguar (BuNo 124435), first flown on 19 May 1952, was the second US variable-geometry design. It used hydraulics to operate the swing-wing mechanism rather than Bell's electrical system. (Grumman Corporation)

The US Navy's emphasis was on developing a subsonic fleet-defender that could loiter for 8 hours over 100 miles from a carrier group, detect incoming bombers or sea-skimming missiles with its powerful AN/APQ-81 pulse-Doppler search radar, and launch its 2,000lb Bendix AAM-N-10 Eagle (later, AIM-54 Phoenix) radar-guided AAMs at six individual targets up to 100 miles distant. It could theoretically destroy supersonic attackers long before shorter-ranged F-4B Phantom II interceptors could be deck-launched. Design proposals included the 70ft-span, 50,000lb Douglas F6D Missileer, with two fuel-efficient, non-afterburning TF30 turbofans developed for the project but later used in the F-111. The Missileer's side-by-side cockpit configuration was reminiscent of that of the A-6 Intruder, in which it was designed to improve crew co-ordination. However, the Missileer's vulnerability due to low speed and poor manoeuvrability plus the cost of its advanced radar and missiles led to its cancellation in 1961.

Instead, the US Navy was persuaded to accept a SOR 183-based proposal as its F-4B Phantom II replacement; and so the seemingly incompatible USAF and US Navy requirements were gradually wrought into the TFX project. Although SOR 183 was still the basis, the US Navy insisted on features that increased TFX's size and weight above the USAF requirements: side-by-side crew positions, carried over from the Missileer cockpit configuration and facilitated by the need for increased internal fuel and a 4ft radar scanner in a wide radome; the crew escape module (giving better chances of survival at sea or in high-speed ejection, but 500lb heavier than ejection seats); and a massive internal missile bay, which might also hold a USAF nuclear warload.

The US Navy had never flown USAF types (apart from the North American F-86 Sabre-derived FJ Fury) from its carriers, so Secretary of Defense McNamara's apparent undermining of its procurement processes in an attempt to 'save a billion dollars', as he put it, upset many within the US Navy, eroded

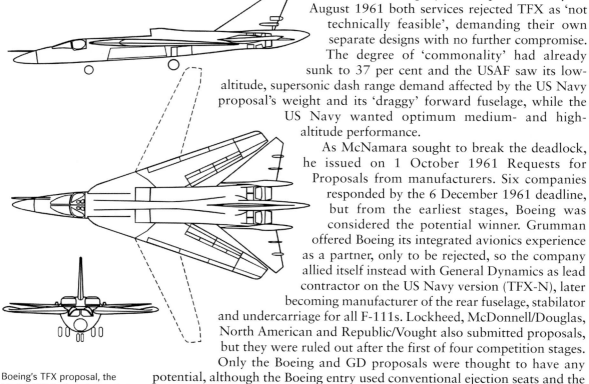

Boeing's TFX proposal, the Model 818, included dorsal air intakes that may have been less effective at high angles of attack, including aircraft carrier landings, than GD's low-mounted inlets. (Boeing)

faith in the TFX project and proved costly. In August 1961 both services rejected TFX as 'not technically feasible', demanding their own separate designs with no further compromise. The degree of 'commonality' had already sunk to 37 per cent and the USAF saw its low-altitude, supersonic dash range demand affected by the US Navy proposal's weight and its 'draggy' forward fuselage, while the US Navy wanted optimum medium- and high-altitude performance.

As McNamara sought to break the deadlock, he issued on 1 October 1961 Requests for Proposals from manufacturers. Six companies responded by the 6 December 1961 deadline, but from the earliest stages, Boeing was considered the potential winner. Grumman offered Boeing its integrated avionics experience as a partner, only to be rejected, so the company allied itself instead with General Dynamics as lead contractor on the US Navy version (TFX-N), later becoming manufacturer of the rear fuselage, stabilator and undercarriage for all F-111s. Lockheed, McDonnell/Douglas, North American and Republic/Vought also submitted proposals, but they were ruled out after the first of four competition stages.

Only the Boeing and GD proposals were thought to have any potential, although the Boeing entry used conventional ejection seats and the unproven General Electric MF295 engine. The company received funding to incorporate the Pratt & Whitney JTF10 turbofan instead.

At the second decision stage on 2 April 1962, both the GD and Boeing submissions were again rejected, but Boeing's remained the most promising. At the third and fourth stages refined proposals from both companies were evaluated, and Boeing's proposal was the clear choice of the USAF and US Navy Selection Board, mainly because it matched the individual services' needs best. McNamara predictably disapproved and on 24 November 1962 he announced that he would personally manage the TFX decision, saying it would be built by GD.

The subsequent furore led to Senate Committee hearings, in which it was suggested that the General Dynamics' Fort Worth facility location in Vice President Lyndon B. Johnson's home state of Texas was a factor among other allegedly fraudulent moves. McNamara's decision was eventually cleared and he justified it by judging that the GD design, though more costly, had 'a very high degree of identical structure for the Air Force and Navy versions. In the Boeing versions less than half of the structural components were the same'. GD's proposal was estimated to offer over 80 per cent commonality, with the differences concentrated in the longer nose area of the USAF version.

As the designers set to work, they faced the constraints of US Navy aircraft carrier deck-lifts, affecting the aircraft's overall dimensions. Height was limited to 16ft 8in and fuselage length to 61ft, including an upward-folding radome, while the USAF's land-based F-111A (as it was renamed in December 1961) was 75ft 6in long. The naval F-111B's wing spanned 70ft (7ft more than the F-111A), reducing to only 34ft when fully swept. Maximum weight was to be 55,000lb for the F-111B and 60,000lb for the F-111A.

GD had a mere 25 months from the 21 December 1962 contract-signing date to complete and fly the first F-111A and many challenges still to confront, particularly those imposed by commonality. More than 6,000 engineers were assigned to the project; and over 20,000 hours of NASA-supervised wind-tunnel tests were required to reach an aerodynamic solution that reduced the severe drag problems (particularly at supersonic speeds) identified in the range of test model configurations. Alarmingly, weight escalation began by the time the mock-up was completed and soon reached 70,000lb.

The first prototype F-111A (63-9766) demonstrates its 72.5-degree wing sweep position at the unofficial roll-out, 22 months after the programme's inception. At the ceremony, Secretary of Defense Robert S. McNamara proclaimed that it had 'the range of a transport, the carrying capacity and endurance of a bomber and the agility of a fighter'. It achieved supersonic speed on its ninth flight on 5 March 1965, reaching Mach 2.03 on 8 August. (General Dynamics)

However, orders had been placed, and GD could only hope to reduce these weight figures during the extremely pressurized prototype evolution using the 18 research and development F-111As, the first of which (63-9766) was rolled out on 16 October 1964, 16 days before the deadline.

General Dynamics also completed ground tests ten days early, and on 21 December 1964 the firm's chief of test flight, Dick Johnson, and engineer Val Prahl took the aircraft on its first flight. This was curtailed by an engine compressor stall during take-off, and an attempt to go supersonic on the second flight (worth a cash bonus) was similarly interrupted by severe stalling in both engines during a straight-and-level flight path. GD's choice of airframe configuration had led to the inclusion of the shortest possible engine intake ducts, using design limits provided by Pratt & Whitney that were based on scanty knowledge of afterburning turbofan characteristics. Compared with an aircraft like the F-4 Phantom II, where long ducts gave the incoming air plenty of distance to achieve a smooth flow even at relatively high angles of attack, the F-111's TF30 front fans were located closer to the intake lips. Although this reduced drag, incoming air hit the compressor blades at a slightly unfavourable angle, particularly during manoeuvring flight, where it could stall, thus potentially causing turbine damage. The prototype was grounded for a month while Pratt & Whitney worked (somewhat acrimoniously) with GD to devise modifications, although these degraded dash speed performance slightly at a time when the F-111 was already being regarded as underpowered. The resultant Triple Plow I intake modifications were introduced in F-111B BuNo 151974 and were followed by the Triple Plow II, tested in F-111A 63-9779.

The eventual proliferation of F-111 sub-types reduced 'commonality', even within the USAF. Rather than the intended production run of at least 1,800 TFXs for USAF, US Navy and foreign users, relatively small batches of land-based variants (usually enough for a single tactical wing) with different, specialized equipment were produced over a ten-year period. This increased unit costs when the inevitable budget overruns on a project with so many unknowns were already attracting intense criticism. Changes were mostly to avionics, concentrated in the forward fuselage section, so that the basic configuration did remain fairly consistent for the 573 airframes manufactured.

'Vark variants

The earliest sub-variant was the RF-111A for which the USAF, which often acquired a photo-reconnaissance variant of each of its tactical fighters, prescribed a highly sophisticated multi-sensor pallet to fit into its weapons bay. Development work was authorized on 3 December 1965, but spiralling costs soon led to cancellation of the project and defeated plans for a wing of RF-111Ds. The reconnaissance modification was later revived for Australia's RF-111Cs.

In December 1965 a strategic bomber version of the aircraft was announced, with potential orders for 263 of this FB-111A model that McNamara wanted SAC to substitute for its Boeing B-52D/F Stratofortress and Convair B-58A Hustler nuclear fleet. The original B-52 replacement, the Mach 3 North American B-70 Valkyrie, had been cancelled in 1961, partly because Soviet advances in missile technology put all high-altitude bombers at risk. However, operating existing bombers at lower altitudes, beneath the defences, made punitive inroads on their range and fatigue lives. The FB-111A, the closest F-111 variant to the original USAF specification, offered long range with a worthwhile payload at safer low altitudes. The F-111A was intended to deliver an internally-carried nuclear weapon over an 800nm combat radius from a low-altitude approach and a 200-mile near-sonic dash to the target. For SAC , the main requirement was longer range and a heavier fuel and weapons load. Contracts were not signed until May 1967 and SAC still hoped for a larger, longer-ranging type as a B-52 follow-on, but did not receive it until the swing-wing Rockwell B-1B Lancer arrived in 1986.

F-111A 63-9776, the only RF-111A, tested the advanced reconnaissance pallet, fitted into the standard weapon bay, between December 1967 and October 1968. Reconnaissance versions of both the F-111A and F-111B were originally required, amounting to 305 examples in all. This F-111A was the last Aardvark with conventional ejection seats. (General Dynamics)

The first FB-111A, displaying Triple Plow I intakes, a SAC 'Milky Way' sash, 600 US gallon external tanks and a nuclear 'shape'. Delivered to the USAF on 30 August 1968, it was employed mainly on test work at Sacramento Air Logistics Center until November 1991. (General Dynamics)

The FB-111A had a new, digital Rockwell bombing/navigation system optimized for nuclear delivery, amongst minimal changes to the basic F-111A; but delays and the rising costs of this system together with McNamara's resignation in 1968 cut the original order for 263 FB-111As to only 76, manufactured between August 1968 and June 1971 at twice the original $6.45m unit cost. Also, incoming President Richard Nixon reinstated the stalled Rockwell B-1 project in 1969, which focused on multi-role capability at low altitude and high subsonic speed but weighed a massive 477,000lb.

Structural alterations for the much smaller FB-111A were limited to a 7ft wingspan increase to 70ft for better cruising speed economy, strengthened landing gear for increased take-off weights up to 109,000lb, and minor redesign of the extreme rear fuselage to house electronics. Extra power was provided by upgraded 20,250lb thrust TF30-P-7 engines. However, considerable changes to the internal avionics eventually pushed the cost of this batch of 76 aircraft well above that of the original order for 263.

FB-111A 67-0163's capacious weapons bay, revealing an AGM-69A SRAM, for which this aircraft was a test-bed in 1969. Four more SRAMs could be carried on underwing pylons. The nuclear-tipped, inertially guided missile had a tiny radar cross-section and radar-absorbent coating, making it virtually invisible to radar during its 110-mile, Mach 3 flight to the target. (General Dynamics)

Sea 'Vark

While the USAF worked on its first two versions, Grumman and the US Navy were experiencing far greater problems with their F-111B, even though Secretary of Defense McNamara had decided to fund 24 F-111Bs within the USAF's budget, making the project more attractive to the US Navy, but also reducing its influence on the project. Airframe changes required for carrier operation included longer, FB-111A-type wings and compatibility with launching and arresting gear. Its weapons system was entirely different from that of the F-111A, but the intended Hughes AN/AWG-9 radar and its 1,000lb Phoenix long-range AAMs were nowhere near ready when the first F-111B flew in 1965. The missile's first unguided launch was made from a Douglas A-3 Skywarrior aircraft on 27 April 1966. Meanwhile, the second

The first F-111B was rolled out in front of a large audience on 11 May 1965 at Grumman's Calverton, Long Island facility, and made its first flight on 18 May 1965 with Ralph H. 'Dixie' Donnell and Ernie von der Heyden in charge. (Grumman Corporation)

and third F-111Bs were stored, awaiting their armament. As the chief of naval operations told a Congressional enquiry that year, 'If the Phoenix missile does not work we do not need the airplane. That is what makes the airplane'. Delays continued and the first Phoenix firing from an F-111B had to wait until March 1967, with a two-year gap until the first double firing, by which time the F-111B programme was dead.

The fourth F-111B (BuNo 151973) was subjected to a 'Super Weight Improvement Program', but overall weight

increased to over 20,000lb above the carrier-operating maximum despite this, partly because of a 10,000lb increase in the internal fuel requirement. Pratt & Whitney proposed a more powerful, lighter and more stall-resistant TF30-P-12 to counter the Naval Preliminary Evaluation (NPE) judgement that the aircraft was 'grossly underpowered'. Relatively slow engine acceleration compared with conventional turbojet power caused concern for carrier approaches, where rapid power increases are essential. The NPE also recommended that the Phoenix missile system's avionics boxes, including an analogue inertial navigation system (INS), should be relocated from behind the cockpit module to a lengthened nose and that the heavy, pivoting missile pylons should be moved to the fuselage. The aircraft's handling on carrier approach was also criticized as visibility over the nose was declared inadequate, requiring the crew seats to be raised 4in and an increase in the windshield angle to 30 degrees for a better view that did not rely on cues from the cockpit's Vertical Display Indicator/Head-Up Display. These changes (the so-called N-1 package, including another 2,000lb of fuel space) were incorporated in the two pre-production F-111Bs (BuNos 152714/715, which also had modified Triple Plow II intakes), the last of the seven F-111Bs to be delivered.

Carrier tests showed the need for a repositioned main landing gear location, combined with the 2ft nose extension, to prevent the aircraft from tipping backwards off the aircraft carrier deck when 'spotted' with its tail over the side. Deletion of the escape module in favour of ejection seats was considered but resisted by the US Navy. Sadly, on 21 April 1967 two test pilots perished when the fourth F-111B, the first to be equipped with the module, crashed at Calverton when the translating cowl intakes closed prematurely on take-off, causing loss of thrust. The crew escape module failed to activate in time, although it went on to demonstrate enviable reliability during USAF service, including the fastest-ever safe ejection (from an F-111D at Mach 2.0).

US Navy opposition to the F-111B increased steadily, fuelled by early tests that showed the aircraft to be inferior in performance in most respects to the F-4B Phantom II that it was intended to replace. It repeatedly failed to meet targets for 'corrective changes', particularly in weight reduction, and it looked increasingly vulnerable to new Soviet fighters, having no real air-to-air capability. Even though the F-111B eventually met its original mission requirements, the perception of that role had changed by 1968 and the project's remaining advocates could no longer muster enough support.

The Phoenix missile, however, was seen as a top priority for fleet defence, but by 1968 the US Navy wanted a more versatile fighter to carry the Phoenix system and also to perform the F-4B's air superiority and escort missions. The result was the VFAX project which eventually led to Grumman being awarded the F-14 Tomcat contract, incorporating the same AWG-9/Phoenix system.

1   F-111A 66-0019, DET 1, 428th TFS 'BUCCANEERS', 474th TFW 'ROADRUNNERS'
During the *Combat Lancer* deployment to Takhli RTAFB, Thailand, November 1968.
2   F-111D 68-0112, 27th TFW, CANNON AFB, NEW MEXICO
At the October 1980 'Giant Voice' bombing competition.
3   F-111E 68-0083 'PROMETHEUS II', 79th TFS 'TIGERS', 20th TFW
At RAF Upper Heyford, UK, 1988.
4   F-111F 70-2366, 366th TFW COMMANDER'S AIRCRAFT
At Mountain Home AFB, Idaho, March 1976.

1

2

3

4

(Not until 1973, in an F-14A, did the AWG-9 radar show that it could take on six separate aerial targets simultaneously, just as the original TFX-N requirement had stipulated.) Lacking support within the US Navy and Congress, the F-111B programme was terminated on 14 December 1968 after $377.7m had been expended on a venture that had, at least, provided useful development of the armament systems, swing wing and engines that would reappear more successfully in the F-14A Tomcat.

F-111D 68-0151 from the 523rd TFS 'Crusaders', 27th TFW with slats and spoilers extended and elevons raised to slow the landing roll without overheating the brakes. Bob Pahl, who flew the D-model for over five years, commented: 'When they had the parts for the avionics and the thing worked, it was a beautiful airplane, the first with a full "glass" cockpit'. (USAF)

As the F-111B faded, the USAF was preparing to combat-test its first operational batch of F-111As in Southeast Asia. Early Category II tests were encouraging, particularly the February 1967 Combat Bullseye series in which the F-111A's all-weather bombing system yielded good results. Engine stalls were still common, but GD was evolving better air intakes. However, cost overruns on a budget that was never sufficient to fund such major technological advances continued to arouse antagonism.

One mishap derived from the novelty of the swing-wing system, manually operated by a sliding pistol-grip control on the pilot's cockpit sidewall. There was much debate among designers about whether it would feel more natural to move the handle forward to go fast (wings swept back) and aft for slower flight (wings extended), or vice versa, sweeping between 16 and 72.5 degrees. On 19 January 1967, F-111A 63-9774 was on approach to Edwards AFB, California at an airspeed suitable for a 16 degrees (extended) wing. At that point, the crew's sweep indicator showed a 26-degree position, and instructor pilot Maj Robert Brightwell momentarily forgot the correct lever operation, pushing it fully forwards. With wings swept back to 50 degrees, the aircraft sank onto the ground a mile short of the runway. Brightwell, relatively uninjured, left the cockpit and attempted to rescue his right-seater, Col Donovan McCance, later the 4527th CCTS Detachment commander. Tragically, Brightwell was standing in leaked fuel that ignited, burning him fatally. The wing-lever movement was subsequently reversed.

Mechanical problems continued. Lt John Nash, a US Navy pilot with two F-4 Phantom II combat cruises in his log-book, was detached to Nellis AFB in Nevada.

I was on an exchange tour in the new and controversial F-111A. I was scheduled to be the commander of the first US Navy F-111B squadron, if the Navy got the aircraft. The Navy dropped the F-111 and I did also after ejecting from one in September 1968.

Flying F-111A 66-0040 with an RAAF pilot, Flt Lt Neal Pollock, Lt Nash was landing the aircraft when the fuel transfer system malfunctioned, moving fuel to the rear of the aircraft and unbalancing it 100ft above the runway. As the aircraft started to roll they ejected; and the crew escape module's parachute opened just in time. Spinal damage took Lt Nash out of the programme and Flt Lt Pollock was 'scared pretty badly', as John recalled it.

There was worse to come, however. In 1968, GD discovered fatigue cracks around bolt holes in the Selb D6AC steel wing carry-through box (WCTB), on which the wings pivoted. All aircraft were limited to 3.5G while 500lb of reinforcing gussets were added to each box at considerable cost. On 22 December 1969, one of the modified F-111As (67-0049) was pulling up from a low-altitude rocket attack on Indian Springs' Range 65 when, as Col Roger Mathiasen recalled,

> The right wing snapped clean off. Right-seater Major Jim Anthony and his pilot [Lt Col Thomas Mack] instantly ejected, but the aircraft had already gone into a violent roll. It hit the ground and the module ejected while inverted, killing both crew members.

This time the cracks had occurred at the wing's pivot-point in the WCTB, and they were caused by a serious manufacturing flaw, not fatigue, in the wing-box. As the weakness had gone undetected by previous inspection methods, it was decided that the work could only be done by proof-testing in very cold conditions. Four costly test facilities were eventually built (including one at BAe Filton, UK for United States Air Forces in Europe (USAFE) F-111E/Fs) where all F-111s were 'cold proof' tested to restore confidence in the structure. Each wing was flexed to +7.3/-2.4G at -40 degrees C while the whole fleet was grounded for seven months, which obviously fed more material to the anti-F-111 lobby. A new, titanium WCTB was developed in 1970 and only three further faults were detected, including one in a tailplane pivot shaft; but periodic, time-consuming cold-proof testing remained part of the F-111 maintenance schedule for the rest of the aircraft's service.

These developments were observed with particular interest by the Royal Australian Air Force. As the F-111's only overseas customer, Australia had ordered 18 F-111As and 6 RF-111As in October 1963 at a substantial discount to replace its Canberra Mk 20 bombers, with the offer of 24 loaned Boeing B-47 Stratojets while F-111 development continued, though this was not taken up. The Mirage IV, A-5/RA-5C Vigilante and F-4C Phantom II were also considered and the Vigilante was initially favoured, but Secretary of Defense McNamara offered far more favourable terms on the F-111A.

By April 1966, with delivery planned for late 1967, it was decided to incorporate the extended wings (to meet the RAAF range requirement) and heavy-duty landing gear of the F-111B/FB-111A under a new F-111C designation, with deliveries from July 1968 and the possibility of using nuclear stores if tensions in Southeast Asia ever became a real threat to Australia. The frustrating structural problems of 1968–69 put the F-111C on hold, however, and the RAAF refused to take delivery of the aircraft until its problems were fully solved. Instead, it received 24 loaned F-4E Phantom IIs as a stop-gap until the first F-111Cs arrived in June 1973. Cancellation of the USAF RF-111A in 1968 also forced the RAAF to adapt its reconnaissance package for its own F-111C to fulfil an important requirement. After this unpromising, costly introduction the F-111C went on to become a highly successful strike/reconnaissance aircraft until its retirement from RAAF service in 2010.

Australia's choice of the F-111 was made against a background of uncertainty about the availability of the British BAC TSR.2 strike aircraft that it had originally considered as a Canberra replacement, though it lacked reconnaissance capability. The British government's cancellation of TSR.2 on 6 April 1965, ostensibly to save £350m, was followed in May 1967 by an order for 50 F-111Ks, provisionally named 'Merlin', for the Royal Air Force. The F-111K

was based on the F-111D (the planned successor to the F-111A), which had an advanced Mk II bombing/navigation system: the world's first production solid-state avionics package designed to deliver conventional ordnance with greater accuracy. Development of the Mk II system was slower and far more costly than anticipated, limiting the majority of the new equipment to the 96 F-111Ds (rather than the 315 plus 60 RF-111Ds originally planned) built from 1972 to 1973. Delays and cost increases exacerbated by an unfavourable dollar exchange rate persuaded the British Labour government to cancel its F-111K order in January 1968, despite incurring £46.4m in cancellation fees.

The F-111E became USAFE's version of the F-111A with Triple Plow II intakes. This example from the 79th TFS, 68-0063 'A Knight to Remember', exhibits the type of commemorative artwork sanctioned by the 20th TFW commander, Col Graham Shirley, from spring 1987 until it was removed during repainting in 1988. (Author)

The basic F-111A analogue avionics were fitted, with some additions, to the next variant, the F-111E. This was an interim model with Triple Plow II intakes and TF30-P-3 engines to keep production flowing while the F-111D's systems were refined. The F-111E entered production in 1969 and ran to 94 copies, almost all of which were based in England with the 20th TFW at RAF Upper Heyford from 1970 to 1993.

Digi 'Vark

F-111D deliveries finally began in November 1971, and the first squadron of the 27th TFW at Cannon AFB reached operational status the following May. The New Mexico-based wing operated most of the production F-111Ds, the only tactical version of the design never to see combat, but potentially the most advanced F-111. Its AN/APQ-130 attack radar made it the only version with real air-to-air capability (the AIM-7G Sparrow medium-range AAM was intended for use with it), although its advanced Norden AN/AVA-9 Integrated Display Set was intended primarily to detect and track airborne threats rather than to attack them. It was also useful for in-flight refuelling. A 1986 proposal to add the PAVE Tack laser and infrared targeting pod was rejected due to electronic complexities.

Lt Col Bob Brotzman was among the early F-111D Weapons System Operators (WSOs).

You had digital computers that provided far more accurate navigation and weapons delivery. They let you install the navigation route before take-off and allowed big excursions from the pre-planned weapon delivery parameters without destroying delivery accuracy. They kept you from going 'heads down' at a low-level-turn-point to dial in the next waypoint or aimpoint, which was not what you wanted to be doing at 200ft and 540kt with people shooting at you. There was an amazing Autonetics inertial platform, the first to use 'wander angle' during ground alignment rather than seeking true north. There was a Canadian Marconi Doppler radar. I always used the navigation mode that mixed the INS and Doppler inputs for computations. It was amazingly accurate, like

These 493rd TFS F-111Fs have a GBU-12D/B Paveway II bomb or two SUU-21/A practice bomb dispensers on their pylons. Major Jim Icenhour flew the F-111F at Lakenheath and thought it was 'a hell of an airplane! It had an ordnance-carrying capacity and internal fuel load that far exceeded any other fighter of the time. It was superb at low level. The faster it went the better it handled. The most impressive thing about the F-111F was its engine thrust. My impression was that the F-111F was like an F-111D with a third engine!' (Jim Rotramel)

you were locked on to some external navigation source. The Autonetics AN/APQ-130 attack radar was phenomenal; better than the F-111A/E and F-111F, though its true resolution was hidden until later years by the [inadequate] analogue signal transfer unit. Then there was the Norden Integrated Display Set. This was magic in its purest form – the first tactical 'glass' cockpit that let you tailor the cockpit displays the way you preferred them. The HUDs (head-up displays) were excellent – really the first of their kind, displaying all sorts of navigation and sensor information. I can remember many occasions coming in to land in rotten weather where the designation cursor on the HUD would lead the pilot's eyes to the runway threshold.

Elements of the Mk II avionics were incorporated in the last main production version, the F-111F, which also fulfilled the long-standing need for a more powerful engine, the TF30-P-100, with faster-running compressors and a new afterburner section yielding over 4,000lb of extra thrust per engine. Delays and cost overruns meant that the F-111D missed this upgrade. Entering service in September 1971, the F-111F flew initially with the 474th TFW (redesignated the 366th TFW in October 1972) at Mountain Home AFB, Idaho before moving to RAF Lakenheath, UK in March 1977. As part of Operation *Ready Switch*, the F-111Fs equipped the 48th TFW in exchange for F-4D Phantom IIs, which were passed to the 474th TFW. The USAFE F/EF-111 force, totalling eight squadrons at its peak, comprised a formidable, all-weather strike force for potential USAFE long-range interdiction missions against Soviet bloc military targets.

During the 1980s, several projects were funded to enhance the capabilities of the F-111 fleet, particularly in the delivery of laser-guided, non-nuclear ordnance. For the F-111F, the Ford Aerospace/Loral AN/AVQ-26 PAVE Tack laser and infrared targeting pod became available in 1980 and equipped the 48th TFW at RAF Lakenheath. The 14ft-long pod, which needed a rotating cradle to support it within the weapons bay and deploy it for use, gave the F-111F's WSO ways of refining final aiming points for self-designating laser-guided bombs (LGBs) both day and night; but, as Jim Rotramel observed, 'The only way [for a WSO] to be good with Pave Tack was to be great with radar'.

PAVE Tack and the F-111F's long range enabled the 48th TFW to launch its *El Dorado Canyon* attack on targets in Libya on the night of 14/15 April 1986, and it was used extensively during the 1991 Gulf War. The retirement of the F-111F force in 1996, after the 48th TFW's conversion to the F-15E Strike Eagle in 1991 and the transfer of its F-111Fs to Cannon AFB for four years of continuation service with the 27th FW in place of its F-111Ds, made PAVE Tack surplus to USAF needs. Ten pods were sold to the RAAF and F-111Cs were modified accordingly.

In 1990 it seemed that the 20th TFW's F-111Es at RAF Upper Heyford would also be updated after 20 years with little modernization. A replacement for the aircraft's original 1965 analogue bombing/navigation system was devised, based on a digital package installed in SAC's FB-111As. The Avionics Modernization Program (AMP) was initiated for the FB-111A in 1986 and was still running when the type was retired from SAC in 1990. However, the axing of the aircraft's basic AGM-69A Short-Range Attack Missile (SRAM) armament and the end of the Cold War made it redundant. Twenty-eight survivors were transferred to TAC as F-111Gs for training duties, and their digital systems and FB-111A structure made them an attractive purchase in 1992 for the RAAF, which bought 15 examples to operate alongside its similar F-111Cs.

The AMP for the F-111E also included a Navstar GPS, two multi-function displays (MFDs) in the cockpit and a new radar display in a programme managed by Grumman and implemented for 25 examples during their programmed depot maintenance (PDM) at BAe Filton, UK or in the USA. However, very few reached the 20th TFW before its F-111Es were phased out in 1993 and returned to the USA. Twenty-four aircraft were reassigned to the 428th FS at Cannon AFB for their last two years of service until October 1995, or sent straight to the Aircraft Maintenance and Regeneration Center (AMARC) in Arizona for storage. (As the 428th TFTS 'Buccaneers', this unit also flew the FS 36118 Gunship Gray-painted F-111G variant in the conventional bombing training role from 1990 to 1993.)

The most radical modification to the FB-111A concept was proposed in July 1977 after cancellation of the Rockwell B-1A. GD developed some of its earlier ideas about an enlarged aircraft, sketched in 1975 as the FB-111G (basically a stretched FB-111A weighing a third as much as the B-1A) and FB-111H. The latter had a fuselage extended to 88ft, but its extra range and payload were still considered inferior to those of the original B-1A. GD persisted and proposed the FB-111B/C, using existing FB-111A and F-111D examples with changes similar to the FB-111H's and the same tandem undercarriage units so that weapons could be mounted on fuselage centreline stations. An extended and widened fuselage would have accommodated 30,000lb thrust General Electric F101GE-100 turbofans. One version (the 'Advanced FB-111') used avionics and a rotary launcher for SRAMs similar to those in later Boeing B-52s. A further development revived the idea of the F-111 as an AIM-54 Phoenix missile platform for ocean patrol, though operated from land bases rather than aircraft carriers. The FB-111B/C competed with a simplified B-1 variant for the USAF's Long Range Combat Aircraft (LRCA) requirement, and in October 1981 President Ronald Reagan announced that 100 B-1Bs would be bought, followed by 150 B-2 stealth bombers. Burgeoning costs reduced the B-2 order to 132 and eventually to just 20 examples.

Spark 'Vark

GD and Grumman reverted to some of the earliest F-111A airframes for a very different version of the F-111, the EF-111A Raven. The USAF's Douglas EB-66 stand-off radar jamming aircraft, vital but slow-moving assets in the Vietnam War, had been retired by 1974; and the Israeli Defence Force/Air Force's experience in the 1973 Yom Kippur War had shown that electronic countermeasures (ECM) pods mounted on tactical fighter-bombers lacked sufficient power to defeat the latest Soviet radars. In the event of European war the USAF would face a daunting electronic scenario, as Lt Gen Robert Mathis pointed out when he unveiled the first EF-111A:

Addition of the 16ft ventral 'canoe', fin-tip 'football' pod and internal countermeasures equipment added over 9,000lb to the EF-111A compared with the original F-111A. Raven 66-0055, seen here with 'Boomerang' artwork (originally worn on a World War II 93rd BG B-24D Liberator) and 42nd ECS markings in 1988, took part in Operation *Proven Force*, flying from Incirlik AB, Turkey. (Author)

> The East European environment today reveals the densest environment of early-warning and ground-control-intercept radar networks known to exist in the world.

No tactical aircraft could carry sufficient equipment to survive those threats while also bearing a useful ordnance load.

Grumman's successful naval EA-6B Prowler was considered, but a faster, longer-ranging aircraft with similar anti-radar capability was preferred. Unlike the EB-66, it would have the performance to penetrate and survive within a hostile aerial environment. The Prowler's Eaton/AIL AN/ALQ-99 jamming suite was modified to fit the F-111A, operated semi-automatically by a two-man crew rather than the Prowler's four. Over 5,500lb of equipment was installed in the F-111A weapons bay and in a 'canoe' fairing beneath it, with radar receiver units encased in a large 'football' fairing (similar to the Prowler's) atop the tail.

Grumman, involved in the F-111 project from the outset, was awarded the conversion contract for 42 F-111As, many of them Vietnam combat veterans, in January 1975. Flight testing with two prototypes began in December 1975 and progressed smoothly, with conversions being delivered until 1985. Performance was similar to that of the F-111A, with up to eight hours 'loiter' time in the threat area. Although empty weight increased by over 8,000lb, removal of the offensive ordnance capability reduced maximum take-off weight by 10,000lb compared with the F-111A. The F-111A's terrain-following radar was retained and the analogue attack radar system (ARS) was upgraded through fitment of the AN/APQ-160 attack radar. Airframe changes focused on the cockpit, the numerous antennas and increased electrical power supply.

EF-111As played key roles in Operation *El Dorado Canyon* and in the Middle East conflicts during the 1990s, scoring very high availability and safety records throughout 17 years of service. One example, 66-016, had been the first F-111A to fly a combat mission during the 1968 Operation *Combat Lancer* deployment. Twenty-three years later, as an EF-111A, it contributed to the destruction of an Iraqi Air Force Mirage F.1EQ, which was probably shot down by an F-15C while pursuing the manoeuvring Raven. Although this was not proof of the F-111's fighter characteristics, it was typical of the many ways in which the soundness of the original design was repeatedly demonstrated during its four decades of service.

TECHNICAL SPECIFICATIONS

Fuselage

The F-111's resin-bonded fibreglass radome housed the attack and terrain-following radar (TFR) antennas. Behind this a large electronics bay contained avionics and circuit breakers for the TFR radar, tactical aid to navigation (TACAN), radio, and identification friend or foe (IFF). In the central fuselage section, a weapons bay was topped by the aerodynamic wing/fuselage 'glove' area. The weapons bay contained a removable gun module, ordnance or a 500lb-capacity cargo platform on an MAU-12 rack.

Crew module

The unique McDonnell-produced, pressurized crew module offered aircrew a 'shirtsleeve' environment and protection when ejecting over land or water. Ejection seats had single-point harness releases, a survival kit in the seat pan and a smaller 'hit-and-run' survival kit if the module landed in hostile territory. Pressurized anti-G suits were worn, but not the usual rubber-lined, anti-exposure 'poopy suits' or bulky parachutes and survival gear. Pulling either ejection handle on the cockpit centre console triggered the complex ejection sequence. Harnesses pulled the crew back into the correct posture and locked. Emergency oxygen was activated, as were a rocket motor, chaff dispenser, and a guillotine and explosive charges to sever the various antennas, power and control connections to the aircraft, including the metal splice plate joining module and fuselage. Air conditioning, pressurization and flying controls had 'quick-disconnect' points. As for comfort, veteran F-111 WSO Maj Jim Rotramel described the cockpit as being 'pretty roomy as fighters go, but still only the size of a sports car – fitted with church pews to sit on, complete with a five-strap seat belt'.

The main 27,000lb thrust rocket motor, with both high-speed and low-speed settings, powered the module upwards, with a counterbalancing upper rocket nozzle. Crews were warned that 'the noise of ejection will be loud but of short duration'. Flt Lt Pete Crowder, who ejected from RAAF F-111C A8-141, described hearing 'a series of metallic clunking noises and then a whoosh with very rapid acceleration'. Cordite fumes filled the cockpit briefly. A 6ft-diameter stabilization brake-chute then deployed, followed by the 70ft-diameter main recovery parachute (automatically opened by a barostatic release below 15,000ft, or manually). An inflatable impact-attenuation bag on the underside softened the module's landing at 29ft/sec. The 'glove' section and extending flaps stabilized the descent.

For water landings, two flotation bags inflated above the glove and self-righting bags were deployed. The control column could be used as a bilge pump (allegedly the right-seater's job!) or to inflate the flotation bags. A damaged module could be kept afloat by pulling the auxiliary flotation handle on the central canopy beam to inflate an air bag on the front bulkhead. Optimum ejection above 2,000ft required 'zooming' the aircraft upwards at less than 300kt for a better module trajectory. At zero altitude and less than 50kt successful ejection was unlikely.

The 'office' of F-111E 68-0069 of the 55th TFS, 20th TFW in July 1993. The left (pilot's) side has many of the F-111A's round 'steam gauges', notably the 11 engine indicators arranged vertically on a grey panel and the larger integrated flight instrument displays to the left of them. To ensure stable low-altitude deployment, the weight differential between the two crew had to be no more than 65lb. (Author)

Communications/avionics

In the F-111E, for example, this comprised an AN/ARC-109 ultra-high frequency (UHF) radio and AN/ARC-123 long-range high frequency (HF) radio, plus an AN/URT-27 emergency radio beacon set. An AN/APX-64 IFF system identified the aircraft to ground stations, while an AN/ARN-52 TACAN received distance and bearing data from ground stations. Instrument landing facilities were provided by an AN/ARN-58 set and an AN/APN-67 radio altimeter gave height-above-terrain information

up to 5,000ft. The AN/AJQ-20 bombing/navigation system worked with the AN/APQ-113 attack radar, the AN/APQ-110 TFR and other inputs, backed up by an AN/ASG-23 gyro-stabilized lead-computing optical sight (LCOS) (or AN/ASG-25 optical display sight (ODS) in later models) for air-to-air and air-to-ground use, or to show homing, navigation or landing information.

Ordnance information for the F-111A/E weapons control system was uploaded via tape cassettes containing coded data and identification for up to 21 different ordnance types, selectable on the weapons control panel. Nuclear weapons were controlled from a separate panel on the WSO's right-seat instrument display, using the same 'permissive action link' (PAL) arming/safety controller as other tactical nuclear aircraft. The attack radar (AN/APQ-113 in the F-111E) had air-to-air and air-to-ground modes, operated with a controller on the right-side cockpit wall and an ARS scope on the WSO's main panel with a detachable hood for daylight use.

The radar offered terrain following (TF), ground mapping (GM) or situation display (SIT) modes. In SIT the crew were shown upcoming obstacles so that they could manoeuvre around them using the landscape to hide from hostile radar. Terrain following could be used manually or automatically, keeping the aircraft at a pre-arranged altitude. It used two antenna receivers located below the ARS dish, deriving information from the radar altimeter, ARS, central air data computer (CADC), flight-control system and other sources. The minimum TFR altitude was 200ft (higher settings were recommended at night or in mountainous areas) and 500ft when used manually in 'E' scope mode. This used 'vertical scanning' by the TFR rather than 'azimuth scan' used in SIT or ground-mapping modes, giving the crew an overall impression of the terrain.

In automatic mode the TFR 'managed' the flight-control system and initiated a 'fly-up' (emergency climb) if the aircraft sank below 68 per cent of its set altitude. Appropriate speed for the conditions had to be maintained or else a fly-up could cause the F-111 to exceed permissible angle of attack (AoA) limits. TFR failure, indicated by a warning light, also triggered a fly-up, as would ascending a long incline with a sudden drop on the other side. A ride-control knob gave the choice of soft, medium or hard ride depending on how closely the flight path followed the terrain and how much negative G discomfort the crew could stand in 'hard' ride, with loose articles flying around the cockpit under negative G. As Col Bob Pahl observed, 'In hard ride you had to have everything strapped down pretty well and soft ride wasn't a good combat setting as the airplane would balloon over crests of hills, like driving a car with too many springs in it'. Medium ride was usually chosen.

Avionics bays occupied the internal area between the radome and the crew module, accessed through lift-up doors. F-111E 68-0035 of the 55th TFS is seen here undergoing programmed depot maintenance. Its nose-art began with the 'Shamrock Kid' name and shamrock leaf in August 1987. The tropical island was added by February 1988. (Author)

TFR imagery appeared on a radar scope above the central instrument display. The system worked effectively in level flight up to 770kt, but initiating a turn directed the aircraft towards terrain that was not being scanned, so that obstacles could go unnoticed at night or in poor visibility. Turns beyond 10 degrees in early F-111s could only be made safely in daylight and were limited to 2 degrees/sec, otherwise TFR could be lost.

Landing gear

Built for aircraft-carrier operations, the Grumman-produced, high flotation landing gear's location in the fuselage was dictated by the variable-sweep wing. The main landing gear (MLG) used a single trunnion with three hydraulic actuators. An aft MLG door was originally attached to the MLG horizontally, but from 1975 it was reattached vertically to the MLG strut. A forward door also acted as a speedbrake below 500kt with the MLG retracted, extending vertically to allow the retracting undercarriage to pass into the well.

Three hydraulic actuators operated the nose-gear, originally designed for F-111B catapult launching. The undercarriage was activated by a control on the landing gear panel, or an emergency pneumatic control. Tyre pressures at 72,000lb take-off weight were 135–145psi (MLG) and 235–245psi (nose-gear). MLG tyres were essentially the same 47×18in 'unprepared airfield' type used on the Lockheed C-130 Hercules, giving up to 100 landings and providing stable carrier landings in F-111B trials. In practice the F-111's 'unprepared airfield' requirement was shelved.

A tail bumper extended beneath the rear fuselage to protect the rear end during over-rotation on take-off or landing. Brakes were hydraulic, multiple-disc types with automatic anti-skid units. Excessive braking could cause the wheel blow-out plugs to vent tyre pressure, and full braking was achieved at about 60 per cent of pedal travel. A 'last resort' arresting hook was available, cleared for standard BAK-9 to BAK-13 runway cable arresting gear.

Fuel system

In-flight refuelling used a floodlit receptacle above the fuselage. Single-point ground refuelling used a receptacle in the left fuselage side, or gravity refuelling through six filler caps above the wings and fuselage. Fuel consumption was managed by a computerized fuel control unit and 12 pumps that initially transferred fuel from external tanks to the forward and aft fuselage tanks, including reservoir tanks and fuel space in the WCTB. There were also two internal wing tanks, two removable weapons bay 'Tokyo' tanks (totalling 585 US gallons but time-consuming to install) and a vent tank in the vertical tail.

B

1   F-111E 68-0068 'THE FLAK DUCKER', 77th TFS 'GAMBLERS', 20th TFW
At RAF Upper Heyford, UK, 1988.
2   F-111F 74-0178, 494th TFS 'PANTHERS', 48th TFW
At RAF Lakenheath, UK, 1992.
3   F-111C A8-147, No 1 SQN, No 82 WING
At RAAF Amberley, Australia, 2002.
4   EF-111A 67-0041 'KNIGHT JAMMER', 42nd ECS 'NATO RAVENS', 66th ECW
At Sembach AB, West Germany/RAF Upper Heyford, UK, July 1987.

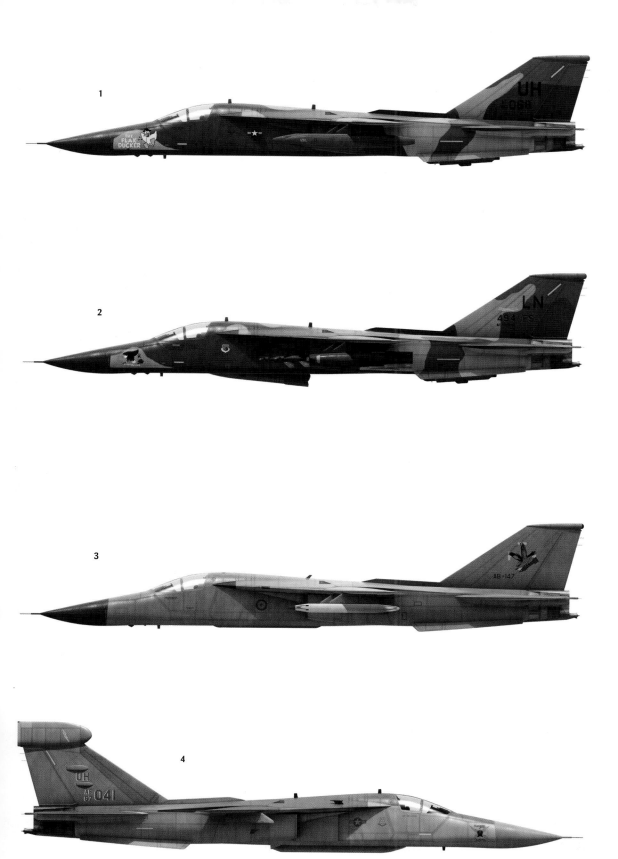

1

2

3

4

External tanks (seldom used by TAC F-111s and never on the 'unplumbed' inboard pylons or on F-111A/Ds) had to be jettisoned in straight-and-level flight at less than 10 degrees' AoA, either when empty or with over 1,800lb of fuel to avoid collision with the aircraft. The FB-111A could carry extra fuel in tanks on the outer, non-pivoting set of pylons, canted inwards at take-off sweep angles.

Engines

Several versions of the Pratt & Whitney TF30 turbofan engine were used by the F-111 fleet, with consequent spares complications. The YF-111A's YTF30-P-1s were soon replaced in the F/EF-111A and F-111C/E by the TF30-P-3, developing 18,500lb thrust in afterburner. These were upgraded for improved reliability to TF30-P-103s, while the F-111D's TF30-P-9s became TF30-P-109s (later retrofitted to EF-111As). The TF30-P-7s used in the FB-111A and F-111G became TF30-P-107s. For the F-111F the TF30-P-100 developed 14,000lb military thrust and 25,000lb in afterburner, over 4,200lb more than previous versions. An MA-1A external pneumatic ground starter was used to start the right engine. Bleed air from this then started the other engine. Two spare cartridges for the alternative cartridge-starting system (for the left engine only) were stored in the MLG well. After landing, the right engine was usually shut down first. Both crew members had throttles, although only the pilot's could be used for engine start and shutdown.

The TF30's front fan section generated a significant proportion of the overall thrust produced by nine low-pressure compressor stages, seven high-pressure stages and eight combustion chambers. Bleed air from the 16th stage provided cooling, pressurization, rain removal and de-icing. Engine nozzles were fully open for minimum thrust with engines at 'idle' power. They closed at higher throttle settings, staying closed except when afterburner was engaged. The shape of the rear fuselage and nozzles contributed over a third of the airframe's total drag, reducing long-range dash – one of the few areas in which the F-111A did not meet its original design requirements.

Five-zone afterburners were ignited by a 'hot streak' ignition system, using 'squirts' of fuel to light the afterburner zones progressively. Extra air was sucked in through six spring-loaded blow-in doors near the rear of the afterburner. Hot gases exited the afterburner at 2,000 degrees F and 1,750mph, creating a hazardous area up to 200ft behind the F-111. A stalled engine fan stage caused an audible bang and needed quick throttling back, when it would either clear or develop into a full engine stall causing a pulsing sensation through the airframe, further bangs and rising engine temperature. Air-starts could be achieved via ram air above 300kt or by cross-bleed air from the other engine below 300kt.

An F-111E's TF30-P-103 engines were accessed via large doors that include the rear ventral fins. The raised structure above the fuselage covers the folded portion of the wing and incorporates the upper section of the fabric wing-seal. Most of the engine auxiliary equipment was located low on the structure for accessibility. (Author)

Air intakes

Operational F/EF-111As, F-111Bs (from BuNo 151974) and all F-111Cs had Triple Plow I intakes with hydraulically 'translating' cowls that slid forward to admit additional air through slots, curved splitter plates and 20 vortex generators, thereby reducing compressor stalls. Landing was feasible with one cowl closed if power on the affected engine was reduced to avoid a stall. Boundary layer diverter air-ducts at the front of the intakes removed low-energy air from below the wing glove and fuselage sides to prevent disturbance to intake air and create an air screen to reduce debris ingestion.

A Triple Plow I intake, used for the F/EF-111A. For the Triple Plow II the structure was moved outwards 3in to control boundary layer air without the curved splitter plate. Development of the TF30 turbofan was one of the costliest parts of the F-111 project. (Author)

An engine technician at work on a TF30. Ground running of the engines was limited to 45 minutes in full military power and only 30 seconds with both engines in zone 4–5 (max) reheat. All TF30s used the same exhaust nozzles apart from the F-1111F's TF30-P-100, which had a slightly different design. During the shutdown procedure, engines were run up to 80 per cent power. When the first TF30 was shut down, hydraulic pressure from the running engine opened the nozzle. However, when the other engine was shut down the hydraulic pressure bled off too fast to open the nozzle. Parked F-111s therefore had one nozzle open and the other closed. (Author)

The Triple Plow I intake was retained for the F-111A, F-111C and the first two FB-111As and then replaced by a complete redesign; Triple Plow II with an 18in-longer 'spike', further reducing engine stalls. At higher speeds the spike expanded, covering a larger intake area to restrict the airflow. Additional air for ground running and low airspeeds entered via three free-floating blow-in doors on each side of the ducts, replacing the translating mechanism. These closed when higher speed 'ram air' effects equalized the pressure inside and outside the intake. The new design improved engine performance at high Mach numbers, and it was used for the FB-111A, F-111D, E and F, with radar-absorbent fibreglass panels inside the intake to reduce frontal radar signature.

Wings

The wings had full-span, double-slotted, trailing-edge Fowler flaps in four interconnected sections acting as one surface. A fifth set (later deleted) was located inboard with a lock to keep the wing at 16 degrees' sweep if they were extended. Each flap had three hydraulic actuators and an air-deflector door extending ahead of it. Four-section leading-edge slats (five on the FB-111A) acted together, driven by flexible shafts, like the flaps. The forward, outer sections of each wing glove rotated downwards to allow full forward movement of the slats. These complex high-lift devices compensated for the F-111's relatively low thrust-to-weight ratio with heavy loads.

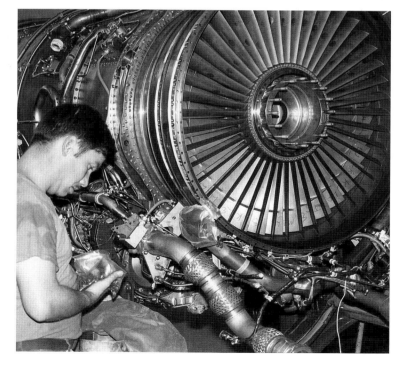

Each wing could flex over 4ft at the tip at high G and minimum sweep. A large fairing and pneumatically inflated seals covered the gaps around the extended inner wing. Spoilers above each wing could be raised hydraulically to 45 degrees to assist with roll control; but only when the wing was at less than 45 degrees sweep, making rolls at subsonic speeds inadvisable at greater sweep angles. All spoilers were raised together to reduce landing ground-roll, assisted by full 'back stick' on the control column to raise the horizontal stabilizers for further air resistance.

Manually-controlled wing sweep was driven by two hydraulic actuators. A sweep-position indicator dial followed the movements of the cockpit sweep-activating handle from 16–72 degrees. A lockout latch on the control handle stopped the wing sweeping beyond 54 degrees aft with weapons on each inboard pylon, thus preventing them from contacting the fuselage. The normal ground-check and take-off sweep position was 16 degrees (with 25 degrees of flaps) and 16–24 degrees for landing. A ground-roll spoiler switch automatically raised the spoilers if throttles were in the idle position with 'weight on wheels', reducing wing lift during landing runs. Normally, sweep positions of 26–50 degrees were used below Mach 0.80. For higher speeds, sweep angles of 45–72.5 degrees were used, depending on stores configuration. A 44-degree setting (allowing use of spoilers for roll control) was favoured for toss-bombing, and 45 degrees for altitudes above 20,000ft for optimum acceleration and AoA. Sweep angles above 50 degrees were normally required for supersonic flight, depending on ordnance loads. Folding the wing back increased the AoA, and vice versa. Wing sweeping could also give rapid acceleration (swept back) or deceleration (swept forward). Stores were carried on four pivoting pylons that aligned with the airstream at any sweep angle. Fixed outboard pylons, used only on FB-111As, aligned with the wings at 26 degrees' sweep.

Hydraulics

F-111s had a primary and secondary system, each with two pumps. Loss of the primary system hydraulic pressure still left flight controls and wing sweep useable, but it also operated slats, flaps, landing gear, nosewheel steering and brakes. Pneumatic systems with two reservoirs drove the tailhook and bumper, emergency systems for the undercarriage, in-flight refuelling, brakes, intake spikes and front-hinged fairings above the wing-fold area.

Flight controls

F-111s had one of the first self-adaptive, triple-redundant stability-augmented flight-control systems. A CADC informed control systems regarding functions such as AoA, temperature and air pressure, as well as monitoring engines, fuel, navigation and TFR inputs. The horizontal stabilizers ('elevons') moved together for pitch control and separately for roll control, replacing the ailerons' function

C **FB-111A 68-0251 'SHY-CHI BABY'**
This aircraft of the 380th Bomb Wing at Plattsburgh AFB, New York, 1988, is seen in the 'Dark Vark' colour scheme (FS 36118 Gunship Gray, FS 34086 Dark Green and FS 36081 Dark Gray) adopted by Strategic Air Command for the aircraft in its low-altitude, nocturnal role. Fairly discreet nose-art was allowed towards the end of the FB-111A's service life, much of it echoing the images used on World War II heavy bombers. 'Shy-Chi Baby' completed 5,539 flying hours before being retired in July 1991, 20 years after the last FB-111A left the production line.

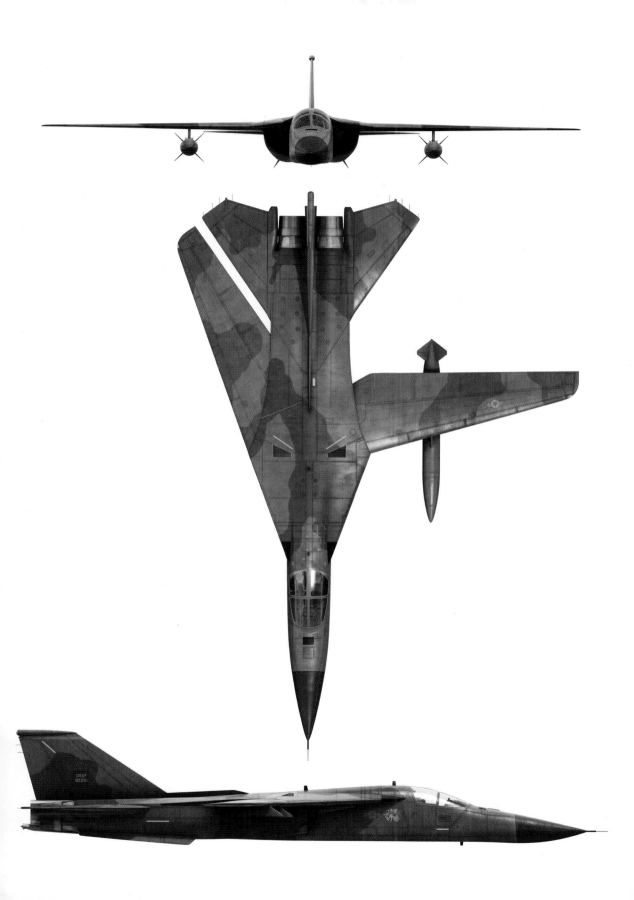

in conjunction with the spoilers. Control surfaces including the rudder were operated by hydraulic actuators connected electrically and mechanically to control columns, the stability augmentation system, autopilot and the TFR. The control column's stick top included buttons for weapons release, trim, nosewheel steering/in-flight refuelling, cannon and autopilot. A unique trim system featured 'series' trim to relieve stick pressure and 'parallel' trim that automatically compensated for wing-sweep changes. Jim Rotramel recalls: 'The only way you could tell if the wing was sweeping was to look outside and watch it – you couldn't sense it'.

Major Jim Icenhour trained at Cannon AFB on the F-111D. 'My first impression of the F-111 was that it was a bitch to land in strong cross-winds, which were routine at Cannon. Like the F-4 [also with naval origins], there was no flare or finesse that one usually associates with a smooth landing. You had to really plant it firmly to get the struts to compress and trigger the spoilers. If you didn't, you could easily lose directional control and scrape a wing-tip, or depart from the runway.' This F-111E has retracted slats and flaps for a 'go-around' in calmer conditions. (Author)

F-111 armament

Cannon

A packaged 20mm M61A1 rotary cannon could occupy the right side of the weapons bay, leaving the other side for ordnance (though almost exclusively in FB-111As). The M61A1's fairing, with automatically opening ports at its front for firing and at the rear for exhaust, replaced the right-side weapons bay doors. Linkless ammunition was stored in a drum housing 2,050 rounds (2,000 useable). Expended cases were returned to the drum. For combat the M61A1 was derated from 6,000 to 5,000 rounds per minute after an explosion in a gun module during tests. Gun-bay vents opened automatically when the M61A1 was fired, and a gun camera and rounds counter were engaged. Designed for strafing, the M61A1 was fired in a 10–15-degree dive angle, although the LCOS 'Gun AA' mode could be engaged for an air-to-air lead pursuit attack. Gun-pod carriage was generally discontinued from 1980 except for some F-111A/Ds, but its previous usage was minimal. Lt Col Edwin Wells, who flew the F-111 with three TAC wings, recalled, 'We had the guns in storage at every base but I never flew an aircraft with one mounted'.

Ordnance

Free-fall weapons of up to 5,000lb could be hung from rectangular MAU-12C/A racks built into the 12S201 or 12S1100 wing pylons, with two more in the weapons bay. Up to six 750lb-class weapons (bomb rack units and multiple ejector racks were sized for M117 bombs) could be mounted on each 10ft-long, streamlined BRU-3A/A (bomb release unit). Bomb release was in symmetrical pairs, outboard to inboard. A cockpit bomb-arm switch allowed nose or tail fuse arming. Early on, F-111As were cleared to carry the 9ft-long 3,000lb M118 GP (general purpose) bomb, LAU-3/A 19×2.75in rocket launcher, BLU-1 (bomb live unit) or BLU-27 fire-bombs, CBU-30 (cluster bomb unit) and CBU-38 cluster bombs (in SUU-13 (suspension underwing unit) downward-ejecting dispensers) and even the CTU-2 resupply pod. However, these weapons were never adopted operationally, although the BLU-27-derived MXU-648 baggage pod was commonly used. The Royal Australian Air Force evaluated a number of stores that never became operational, including the Karinga CBU, AGM-88 HARM, AIM-132 ASRAAM, AGM-158 JASSM, GBU-15, GBU-31 and GBU-38 JDAMs (Joint Direct Attack Munition). The following weapons were used operationally:

The 750lb-class **M117 GP warhead** (originally called a demolition) was filled with 386lb of Tritonal and could be fitted with three fins. The original M131 conical fin was used for the *Combat Lancer* Vietnam deployment, as was the MAU-91 retard fin for the M117R. The M117D air-laid bottom mine used a Mk 75 Destructor kit comprising a Mk 32 arming device with a Mk 42 firing mechanism. After Vietnam, the MAU-103 conical fin replaced the M131, but the M117 soon became a B-52-only weapon. Length: 7ft 6in; diameter: 16in.

The 500lb-class **Mk 82 warhead** was filled with 192lb of Tritonal explosive. A cast-concrete training substitute was the blue BDU-50. For the F-111, Mk 82s could be fitted with three fins. Mk 82 low-drag general-purpose bombs (LDGPs) had MAU-93 conical fins, as used for *Constant Guard V* missions in Vietnam, particularly for *Combat Skyspot* missions, with 24 per aircraft. The US Navy-developed Mk 15 Snakeye retard fin was preferred for low-altitude TFR deliveries, with six per outboard BRU-3A/A. It slowed the bomb to detonate well behind the aircraft but forced the F-111 to fly at less than 500kt, far below its maximum speed. Fitted with the Mk 75 kit it became the Mk 36 Destructor. To overcome the Snakeye's speed limitations, the BSU-49 AIR (bomb stabilization unit, air inflatable retard) fin with a 'ballute' (balloon/parachute) retarding unit, allowing delivery at 600kt, was introduced operationally in early 1986 and used in Operation *El Dorado Canyon*. Length: 7ft 6in; diameter: 10.75in.

The 2,000lb **Mk 84 warhead** contained 945lb of Tritonal. A BDU-56 training version had a cast-concrete 'warhead'. Mk 84s could use two fins: the Mk 84 conical fin for the LDGP version, used for early *Constant Guard V* missions; and later the BSU-50 'ballute' for low-altitude, high-speed delivery. With the Mk 75 kit the bomb became the Mk 41 Destructor, though only the F-111C was authorized to use this. Length: 13ft; diameter: 18in.

Although all F-111s could deliver **laser-guided bombs** (LGBs), only the F-111C and F-111F could do so autonomously. The original PAVE Way I LGBs, identifiable by their fixed wings, saw limited use in F-111 training in the early 1980s. They combined the MAU-157 guidance kit with the KMU-351 (Mk 84 LGB or GBU-10/B, A/B or B/B) or KMU-388 (Mk 82 LGB or GBU-12/B or A/B) modification kits that included the canards, wings and warhead-to-guidance section adapter collar. However, the F-111 used the folding-fin

The F-111's extensive weapons bay, looking forwards, with an MAU-12 weapons rack to the left and the compact M61A1 Vulcan cannon package on the right with its air and gun-gas vents. Col Larry Peters also found that the F-111F was actually a very capable gun platform when delayed OT&E (operational test and evaluation) tests took place in 1974, though it was never proven in combat. 'I can honestly say that the F-111F was the best strafing aircraft that I ever flew.' He also rated it against towed air-to-air dart targets when used with the F-111F radar's air-to-air mode. (Jim Rotramel)

Mk 82 AIR bombs on the BRU-3A/A of the 20th TFW's 'The Chief'. With six bombs on stations 3 and 6 (the outer pylons), bomb collision after release could occur, so a 'train' release was best, dropping symmetrically from both sides and keeping the release button pressed long enough to release all stores from the chosen stations. (Author)

29

Hefty 2,000lb GBU-24 Paveway IIIs aboard a 48th TFW F-111F. PAVE Tack was normally extended from the open weapons bay when the aircraft was parked, but with its seeker head swung to one side to protect its sensor window. F-111s could also use the 2,000lb Mk 84 AIR 'lay-down' weapons, whereas the low-drag general purpose (LDGP) version required a very rapid climb to escape debris damage. (Author)

Paveway IIs, introduced in 1977 with the improved MAU-169 guidance section with the MXU-651 (GBU-10C/B, D/B or E/B) or MXU-650 (GBU-12B/B, C/B or D/B) airfoil groups. The latter version of these weapons saw extensive use in operations *El Dorado Canyon* and *Desert Storm*. Introduced in the mid-1980s, the BLU-109 2,000lb penetrating warhead held only 535lb of Tritonal. It too saw use during *Desert Storm*, with F-111Fs using the same MXU-651 (GBU-10G/B, H/B or J/B). Length: GBU-10 14ft 2in; GBU-12 11ft.

The **Paveway III** low-level laser-guided bomb (LLLGB) became operational in 1986 after *El Dorado Canyon* and had better low-altitude launch performance and a more sophisticated WGU-12 proportional guidance system and BSU-94 airfoil group, providing a 10-mile stand-off capability compared with 2 miles for Paveway II. F-111Fs used both Mk 84 (GBU-24/B) and BLU-109 (GBU-24A/B) variants of Paveway III extensively during *Desert Storm* and also two 4,700lb GBU-28/B 'bunker buster' LGBs with BLU-113 warheads on the last night of the war. Length: GBU-24 14ft 2in; GBU-28/B 19ft 1in.

The Mk 84 and BLU-109 were used for yet another application: the 2,500lb **GBU-15 PAVE Strike** modular guided weapon system (MGWS) stand-off glide-bomb and its rocket-powered derivative, the AGM-130. Both were guided by a Hughes AN/AXQ-14 datalink pod on the F-111F's rear station. The Mk 84-based versions were the TV-guided GBU-15(V)-1/B and the imaging infared (IIR)-guided GBU-15(V)-2/B, both with long-chord MXU-74 wings. The BLU-109-based bombs were the TV-guided GBU-15(V)-31/B and IIR-guided GBU-15(V)-32/B, both with short-chord MXU-787 wings. The 3,000lb, Mk 84-based AGM-130A and BLU-109-based AGM-130C served briefly with the F-111F. Length: 12ft 11in. The AGM-142E Popeye/Raptor medium-range stand-off missile was evaluated on the F-111F in 1988 but used only on the F-111C from 1993 with its AN/ASW-55 datalink pod.

 D

ARMAMENT AND OTHER STORES

1. B61 nuclear weapon
2. GBU-28 'bunker buster'
3. GBU-15
4. GBU-12 LGB
5. GBU-24/BLU-109/B Paveway III
6. GBU-10 Paveway II
7. Mk 82 AIR

8. CBU-87 CEM
9. AIM-9P Sidewinder
10. AGM-84 Harpoon
11. AGM-142 Raptor
12. AVQ-26 PAVE Tack
13. AN/ALQ-119 ECM pod
14. AN/ALQ-131 ECM pod

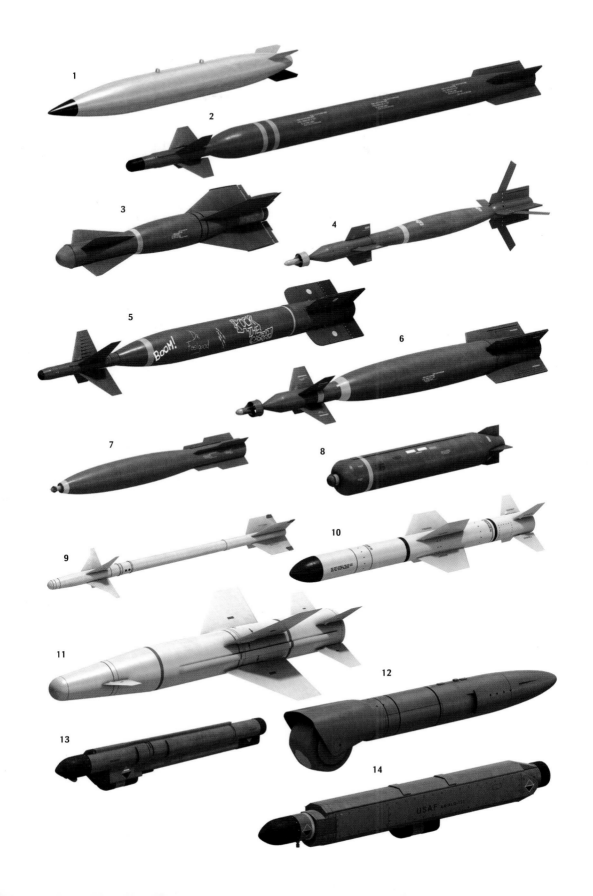

BLU-107 **Durandal** runway-denial munitions were briefly used with F-111Fs. The F-111 used the CBU-58/B cluster bomb in combat. It was a SUU-30B/B dispenser, loaded with BLU-63 fragmentation bomblets, and was used during *Constant Guard V* and in Operation *Proven Force* as the CBU-58B/B and CBU-71B/B (with delayed-action BLU-86 bomblets). Length: 7ft 8in; diameter: 16¼in.

NATO **BL755** cluster bombs were also available to USAFE in an emergency. Mk 20 Rockeye II cluster bombs were for maritime tactical support (attacking Soviet warships) and some were dropped by F-111Es during Operation *Proven Force*. The RAAF used the AGM-84 Harpoon missile for anti-shipping purposes.

The 800lb-class **tactical munitions dispenser** (TMD) was a family of CBUs too large for BRUs but pylon-mounted for both F-111Es and F-111Fs during the Gulf War. CBU-87 combined effects munitions (CEMs) used BLU-97 sub-munitions in an SUU-65 dispenser, while the CBU-89 Gator mine was mainly armour-piercing, with 72 BLU-91 anti-tank mines and 22 BLU-97 anti-personnel mines. Length: 7ft 8in; diameter: 17in.

Nuclear weapons

SAC FB-111As carried the B61 or B43 'special' (nuclear) weapon on their inner wing pylons or in the weapons bay. Alternatively, two 2,230lb AGM-69A SRAMs with W69 nuclear warheads went into the weapons bay and on two on the inner pylons. TAC and UK-based F-111E/Fs could carry B53, B57 or B61 nuclear bombs on their inner pylons or in the weapons bays. US-based F-111A/D/Gs were not nuclear-capable.

For weapons training, US-based and RAAF F-111s used either the SUU-20 practice bomb/rocket dispenser with six 25lb blue BDU-33 low-drag practice bombs, or 10lb orange Mk 106 high-drag practice bombs (not used by the RAAF) held in place by 'ice tong' clamps and tubes for four 2.75in rockets, which were never used. European-based F-111s used the cylindrical SUU-21 with the same bombs. These dispensers were always mounted on the inboard pylons and on weapons training detachments (WTDs) BRU-3A/As might be hung on the outer pylons too, for carrying Mk 82s.

Air-to-air missiles

During *Combat Lancer*, F-111As carried a single AIM-9B Sidewinder AAM on an AERO-3B launcher attached to a retractable trapeze in the left side of the weapons bay, but AIM-9Bs were probably not loaded during *Constant Guard V*. In the mid-1970s the AERO-3Bs were upgraded to LAU-105 standards, and captive versions of the AIM-9E and AIM-9P were sometimes used for familiarization training, with the launcher mounted on an adaptor on the outboard side of the outer pylons (stations 3A and 6A). Air combat manoeuvring instrumentation (ACMI) pods could also be fitted to 3A or 6A for range work, such as *Red Flag*. The adapter mounting only suited these 'small-wing' AIM-9s; later 'big-wing' AIM-9L and AIM-9M versions were mounted on the bottoms of the pylons on LAU-105s. AIM-9Ps were carried for the first two nights of Operation *Desert Storm*.

Electronic countermeasures

ECM pods were utilized on all F-111s except the EF-111A, FB-111A and F-111G. Vietnam War F-111As toted pairs of AN/ALQ-87s beneath the weapons bay and rear fuselage. Combinations of two AN/ALQ-87(V)-2s were used during *Combat Lancer*, while AN/ALQ-87(V)-1 and (V)-2 (also (V)-3 or (V)-2 and (V-)4) on the forward and rear stations were common during *Constant Guard V*. After Vietnam the rear-mounted, 13ft-long AN/ALQ-101(V)-2 or (V)-3 was used, replaced in the late 1970s by the aft-mounted 9ft 3in-long AN/ALQ-119(V)-14 or (V)-17. In the early 1980s the 9ft 3in-long, 20in-deep 'shallow' AN/ALQ-131 pods were provided for UK-based F-111E/Fs. Normally aft-mounted, the pod was hung on the closed PAVE Tack cradle when GBU-15s or AGM-130s were carried, as an AN/AXQ-14 datalink pod occupied the rear station. Having a contingency mission, Cannon-based F-111Ds had the 11ft 11in-long QRC 80(V)-3. F-111Cs used the IAI ELTA-8222 jamming pod on the aft or right-wing inboard station.

F-111 dimensions			
Variant	Wingspan (at 16 and 72.5 degrees sweep)	Length (including pitot)	Height
F/YF-111A/D/E/F	63ft/32ft	73ft 6in	17ft 1in
EF-111A	63ft/32ft	73ft 6in	20ft
FB-111A/F-111C/G	70ft/33ft 11in	75ft 6in	17ft 1in
F-111B (pre-production)	70ft/33ft 11in	68ft 10in	15ft 9in

Weights (lb)					
Variant	Empty	Basic	Combat*	Max take-off	Max landing
F-111A	42,200	49,310	59,620	92,500	72,000
EF-111A	53,600	55,275	61,729	87,800	80,000
FB-111A	45,200	49,090	70,380	114,300	82,000
F-111B	46,112	54,563	68,165	77,566	56,980
F-111C	47,300	50,000	70,000	114,300	82,000
F-111D	46,900	50,294	61,930	92,500	72,000
F-111E	45,700	49,310	59,620	92,500	72,000
F-111F	47,481	51,190	62,350	100,000	72,000
F-111G	45,000	48,813	88,813	114,300	80,000

*basic combat configuration

Production numbers			
Variant	Serials	Number built	First flight
RDT&E F-111A	63-9766 to -9783	18	21 December 1964
Pilot production F-111A	65-5701 to 66-0012	12	12 February 1967
Production F-111A*	66-0013 to 67-0114	129	24 September 1967
FB-111A	67-0159 to 69-6514	79**	30 July 1967
F-111B	BuNos 151970 to 152717	9†	18 May 1965
F-111C	A8-125 to A8-148††	24	28 August 1968
F-111D	68-0085 to 68-0180	96	15 May 1967
F-111E	67-0015 to 68-0084	94	20 August 1969
F-111F	70-2362 to 74-0188	106	August 1971

*42 F-111A from serial batch 66-0013 to 67-0052 converted to EF-111A and four transferred to RAAF

** includes two RDT&E and three static test airframes. Thirty-four modified to F-111G and 15 of these transferred to RAAF

† last two not completed

†† US serials 67-0125 to 67-0148

F-111 VARIANTS AND MODIFICATIONS

YF-111A

The first 12 aircraft had individual differences in their fuel control/distribution systems, fire-detection sensors, gravity refuelling, hydraulic accumulators, nosewheel steering and rotating wing gloves. Instrument panels had many more round dials than later variants and the seats were Douglas Escapac standard rocket catapult ejection seats, cleared for 400kt maximum speed at 300–400ft minimum altitude. For the first 11 aircraft, the entire canopy was jettisoned when the ejection face-screens were pulled down. Three sets of spoilers were installed. In December 1966 the YF-111A still had long-range, high-altitude interception with air-to-air missiles as a primary mission, and its armament reflected this. Two hydraulic AIM-9B Sidewinder trapeze launchers (later deleted) were located side-by-side in the weapons bay, deploying when

F-111A 67-0038 in the markings of the 4527th CCTS. It entered USAF service in August 1968 and was converted into an EF-111A in 1984, flying with the 366th TFW and 42nd ECS, including Operation *Desert Storm* missions. In December 1991 its wing carry-through box (WCTB) failed during 'cold proof' load testing at McClellan AFB. The pattern of red lines behind the crew module assisted the aim of the aerial refuelling tanker boom operator. (USAF)

the weapons bay door opened. Six more AIM-9B AAMs could be launched from wing pylons. Test weapons loads included four AGM-45A Shrike anti-radiation missiles, AGM-12B Bullpup air-to-ground missiles (trapeze- or pylon-mounted) and SUU-16A 20mm gun-pods, firing with the internal gun.

YF-111As tested the operational AN/AJQ-20 bombing/navigation system. The third aircraft, 63-9768, was still in service as an RAAF ground instructional airframe in 1998. Two RDT&E aircraft (63-9771/-9777) joined NASA's Dryden Flight Research Center to develop Triple Plow intakes in 1967; and 63-9778 explored transonic aircraft technology (TACT) with the supercritical wing, which greatly improved F-111 performance, and the mission adaptive wing as part of the Advanced Fighter Technology Integration (AFTI) research programme from 1984 to 1987. The AFTI wing dispensed with conventional flaps and slats, flexing and changing its aerofoil shape according to airspeed. F-111A 66-0011 was modified with FB-111A electronics and used for SRAM tests. Ten pre-production F-111As were offered to the RAAF in 1980, but were considered too incompatible with the F-111C/G.

F-111A

This, the first operational version, served with two TAC wings successively and some examples outlived later variants after conversion to EF-111As, or F-111Cs for the RAAF. F-111A 66-053 tested the Norden/Grumman synthetic-aperture radar battlefield surveillance system in the 1982 Pave Mover programme. Nine F-111As were lost in combat and another 35 in training accidents, at least 11 of these due to engine fires or hydraulic problems. Post-Vietnam, F-111As continued in service with the 474th TFW, but were transferred to the 366th TFW at Mountain Home AFB in August 1977 when that wing's F-111Fs were moved to USAFE. They continued as trainers until spring 1992. Col Bob Brotzman commanded the 391st TFS at the base in 1986.

> By then most of the hysteria regarding the F-111 had died down and it was just seen as a versatile aircraft with a long range and a big bomb load. We spent a lot of time working on daytime tactics, and even medium-altitude formation tactics and the whole 'night/low-level/single ship' thing had been gotten into perspective. We did a lot of composite force training where we would fit into a mixed bag of other fighters in big raids.

NF-111A 63-9778 was a pre-production F-111A, extensively modified with a supercritical wing in 1973 as NASA's Transonic Aircraft Technology (TACT) test aircraft and remodelled again in 1986 with a variable-camber, 'mission adaptive' wing as the Advanced Fighter Technology Integration (AFTI) test aircraft. The wing dispensed with conventional flight controls and reshaped its own aerodynamic cross-section to change the aerofoil profile for different speed requirements. (NASA)

EF-111A

The aerodynamic test aircraft (F-111A 66-049) first flew on 10 March 1977; and 66-041 followed, testing the Eaton AIL AN/ALQ-99E jamming sub-system, with ten antennas in the underfuselage 'canoe' and receivers in the fin-top 'football'. The first production aircraft (66-049 after modifications) was rolled out on 19 June 1981. Forty-two early production F-111As with around 2,000 flight hours each were selected for conversion. About a quarter of the F-111A airframe needed changes, including a strengthened rear fuselage to handle 800lb of extra sensors in the 'football' and fin-side fairings. A large detail display indicator (DDI) occupied much of the right-seat front instrument panel, and the other right-seat displays and controls were moved to the centre of the front panel. The right-seat control column was removed and a radar/threat monitoring control console was fitted. 'Bullet' antennas for the AN/ALQ-137 receiver and AN/ALR-62 forward radar warning receiver were scabbed on above the wing root, and AN/ALQ-99 antennas protruded beneath the wing root and from the tail-fin. The 388th ECS 'Griffins' under the command of Lt Col Tom Pickering was first to receive EF-111As (starting with 66-0051 on 5 November 1981), having already worked up with the two prototypes.

EF-111A 66-037 shows the plethora of additional antennas needed for its job, the unique, robust undercarriage structure and the distinctive 'aardvark ears' canopy sections. This was the first EF-111A for the 42nd ECS, and it completed 49 missions during Operation *Desert Storm*. (Author)

RF-111A

The 11th test aircraft (63-9776) successfully tested the reconnaissance pallet in December 1966, and $116m was spent on developing infrared and sideways-looking radar sensors, cameras and a digital management system. This aircraft flew on 17 December 1967, but it was clear that the pallet could never be a 'quick conversion', plug-in component as it took two days to install. A proposal for 60 RF-111Ds was cancelled and replaced by one to convert 46 (later 24) F-111As for reconnaissance. This too was cancelled in March 1970 and the USAF stuck with its RF-4C Phantom IIs. An RF-111B version was also proposed in November 1966.

FB-111A

The prototype (F-111A 63-9783) exceeded Mach 2 on its first flight and the first pre-production FB-111A (67-0159) flew on 13 July 1968. FB-111A 67-0161, delivered in June 1969, was the first with Triple Plow II intakes, TF30-P-7 engines and Mk IIB avionics. The lengthened wings were 'plumbed' for six external tanks rather than the usual four. Internal tanks were enlarged to cope with a range reduction caused partly by the use of Triple Plow II intakes. Initial SAC plans for 14 squadrons plus 20 trainers (263 aircraft in total) were cut to 128 aircraft on 28 November 1968 and then to 76 in March 1969.

The AGM-69A SRAM missile, a primary FB-111A weapon from 1973, required a control panel in the cockpit. From 1977 aircraft had AN/APX-78 I-band radar transponders so that ground I-band stations could track them, AN/ARN-84(V) TACAN with 126 channels and an AN/APX-64 five-mode Mark X IFF system. The AN/APQ-114 attack radar offered three ground modes for mapping, fix-taking and weapon delivery and an air-to-air mode that was used only for tanking and aircraft identification. An AN/APQ-134 TFR was installed. Radar homing and warning (RHAW) included a fin-tip AN/AAR-34 rear-warning unit. Penetration aids included a countermeasures dispenser (CMDS), ECM, and an infrared receiver (IRRS). An F-111 AMP was begun in December 1986, initially with the FB-111A, to improve reliability. It included a ring-laser gyro-driven inertial navigation set, two MFDs for the navigator, a new bombing/navigation system computer and a data transfer module for loading flight plans. The TFR was revised and a new digital databus was installed.

F-111B

The US Navy's TFX, first flown on 18 May 1965, had the TF30-P-1 until more powerful TF30-P-12 engines became available in late 1966. Each of the first three prototypes had Escapac ejection seats and only one control column. A nose-tow catapult launch bar was added to the nose landing gear. F-111Bs pioneered the use of cockpit CRTs, using experience gained with the Kaiser units in Grumman's A-6 Intruder. The AWG-9 track-while-scan radar system and datalink for automatic interception control was extremely advanced, although it lacked manual reversion.

During 23–24 July 1968 carrier trials onboard USS *Coral Sea* with BuNo 151974, the fourth F-111B, the prototype demonstrated pleasing handling characteristics; but the aircraft's burgeoning weight and logistics demands were seen as insoluble problems even without the additional burden of its six Phoenix AAMs and other armament. The two pre-production aircraft (BuNos 152714/715), which had a version of the Triple Plow II intakes, a 2ft nose extension, an infrared seeker below the nose and a slightly raised canopy profile, continued Phoenix missile trials until 1971.

F-111C

This RAAF variant first flew in August 1968 and was ready for delivery in September, but was delayed due to the F-111A's wing-box problems. RAAF personnel flew to collect them in December 1969, but the discovery of further wing problems caused a return to storage and the possibility of cancellation. Finally, delivery began from 1 June 1973.

The F-111C was basically an F-111A with extended FB-111A wings, a stronger undercarriage and a removable right-seat control column. F-111Cs were modified to take PAVE Tack and AGM-84A Block IC or AGM-84D Harpoon data-linked, sea-skimming missiles. Much of the Avionics Update Program (AUP) was delegated to Australian companies from 1994 under contract to Rockwell Autonetics, and completed in 1999. A Honeywell digital flight control system used multi-function CRT displays. The first AUP aircraft (A8-132) was upgraded by Rockwell Autonetics in the USA; the rest in Australia by Hawker de Havilland and maintained by No 501 Wing RAAF. Improving upon the USAF's AMP, the AUP included TFR upgrades to

F-111C A8-144 from No 1 Squadron, No 82 Wing, RAAF visits Boscombe Down, UK for the TVS Show in June 1990. Australian 'Pigs' and 'Photo Pigs' defended the 'moat' around their country from 1973 until 2010. They were progressively updated to accept PAVE Tack, AGM-84 Harpoon, GBU-15 and AGM-142 Have Nap. (Author)

AN/APQ-171B standard, uprated Martin Marietta AN/APQ-169 attack radar, a Honeywell AN/ASN-41 ring-laser gyro INS, MAG-R GPS, a new stores management system with a more powerful IBM AP-102A mission computer, KY-58 secure voice, Have Quick UHF radios and an FS 36118 Gunship Gray paint scheme. There were also important upgrades to the electronic warfare self-protection (EWSP) suite. AGM-88 HARM anti-radiation missiles were tested on the Aircraft Research and Development Unit's (ARDU) F-111C but not purchased. External fuel tanks were regularly carried. A series of block upgrade programmes (BUPs) added to AUP improvements, including upgraded CMDS, radar warning receiver (RWR) and additional stand-off attack capability; but these remained conjectural, as retirement of the F-111C from RAAF service was brought forward to 2010 after recurring wing fatigue failures (requiring wings from stored F-111Fs to be obtained from AMARC); and the Lockheed Martin F-35A Lightning II was ordered, with F/A-18F Super Hornets as an interim purchase.

RF-111C

Despite the USAF's cancellation of the RF-111A, Australia approved in July 1977 the conversion of F-111C A8-126 by GD to an RF-111C in 1978, with two KS-87C split-vertical framing cameras, one KA-56E low-altitude panoramic camera, one KA-93A4 high-altitude panoramic camera and an AN/AAD-5A infrared line-scan and a TV viewfinder. Full underwing ordnance capability was retained and Harpoon anti-ship missiles could be carried after the AUP. Three more RF-111C conversions were carried out by No 482 Sqn and No 3 Aircraft Depot RAAF using GD kits. A Raytheon DB-110 podded reconnaissance system was flight-trialled on RF-111C A8-134 in 1999.

F-111D

Essentially an F-111E airframe with Mk II avionics and improved TF30-P-9 engines, the first production example (68-0085) flew on 15 May 1970. The F-111D was originally intended to carry the AIM-7 Sparrow medium-range AAM and the self-testing AN/APQ-130 attack radar in its very advanced

Mk II avionic system, which provided continuous-wave illumination to guide this type of missile as well as detecting and tracking air and moving ground targets. The Mk II system used two head-up displays (HUDs), a CRT display on the pilot's side and a large radar display for the WSO with a bigger TFR scope, all linked to other sensors via a new IBM AN/AYK-6 digital computer complex. Either crew member could fly the aircraft and operate its weapons systems. The Mk II system experienced long development delays (particularly the Norden integrated display set) that were only fully resolved late in the F-111D's career. Efforts to upgrade the D-model with LANTIRN targeting pods and make it compatible with TV-guided weapons failed to receive funding, and in 1991 it was among the first F-111 variants to be withdrawn.

F-111E

Making its first flight on 20 August 1969, the F-111E was similar to the F-111A with Mk I avionics but Triple Plow II intakes. Equipment included a KB-18A strike camera, AN/APQ-110 TFR and AN/APQ-113 attack radar, but the F-111E never received PAVE Tack. AMP updates made the F-111E and F-111G cockpits very similar. The AN/ALE-28 countermeasures dispenser was replaced by a Tracor AN/ALE-40 with 30 RR-170 chaff cartridges and 15 MJU flares.

F-111F

This ultimate version combined elements of F-111D and FB-111A avionics such as the Mk IIB set, with F-111E-type cassette-based stores management systems, AN/APQ-144 attack radar without Doppler filters or moving target indicator (MTI), AN/APQ-146 TFR and TF30-P-100 engines. The original order for 219 was cut to 82, but follow-on batches of 24 (12 in March 1971 and 12 in July 1972) took the total to 106. The F-model had a Rockwell INS, a general navigation computer (GNC) feeding a display on the right-seat instrument panel and a weapons delivery computer (WDC) holding data on all the aircraft's possible weapons loads. Wing-box problems were minimized by a new 'safe life' version.

The introduction of the AN/AVQ-26 PAVE Tack targeting pod greatly enhanced the F-111F's all-weather strike capability. The pod incorporated an AN/AAQ-9 forward-looking infrared (FLIR) with gallium-arsenide aperture and a laser ranger and designator. Imagery was displayed on a virtual image display (VID); this featured two video displays, which behind a large magnifying glass appeared to be a 6in screen above a 3in screen, allowing the WSO to swap ARS and FLIR video between the two screens thus enabling him to control the sensor in the top screen while being able to observe the other sensor in the lower screen. In all, 85 F-111Fs and 17 F-111Cs received the cradle installation for PAVE Tack, which rotated the 1,385lb unit through 180 degrees, extending it through a cut-out in the weapons bay doors. On its cradle the pod could rotate left and right and its seeker head could swivel fore and aft. A WSO could monitor radar and PAVE Tack imagery simultaneously on his VID, although the pod's field of vision was too narrow for navigation. When extended, its drag factor increased fuel consumption by only about 2 per cent. Before take-off, a WSO could 'boresight' the pod on a suitable ground object to check it was functioning and then retract it for take-off.

Some F-111Fs were equipped with the AN/AXQ-14 datalink pod for GBU-15 electro-optical glide-bombs. From 1989 the F-111F's computer complex was upgraded, and the previous punched-tape mission loading system was replaced by a portable digital mission data loader that gave a much more flexible means of entering mission navigation data. A final update in the mid-1990s, Rockwell's Pacer Strike programme, gave 28 F-111Fs at Cannon AFB streamlined flight-control systems, MFDs and an INS integrated with Navstar GPS. Improvements in reliability and maintainability were considerable, but the F-111's withdrawal from service was imminent and the programme was curtailed.

F-111G

From early 1989, 34 FB-111As (replaced in SAC by the Rockwell B-1B) were converted to F-111Gs as conventional armament trainers for the 27th TFW. SRAM capability was removed together with SAC's satellite communications system, and the weapons delivery system was optimized for conventional capability but not LGBs. F-111Gs had an AN/ALE-40(V) countermeasures dispenser system and TF30-P-107 engines. A Have Quick II AN/ARC-164 frequency-hopping secure UHF radio and an AN/ARC-190(V) HF radio were installed together with an AN/ARN-118 TACAN, and two MFDs for navigation and bombing data display for dive, level and toss-bombing modes. The airframe was beefed up to tolerate 6.5G. Plans to convert 12 aircraft annually were curtailed, and a proposal to upgrade the others into 'Wild Weasel' surface-to-air missile (SAM) suppression and electronic reconnaissance aircraft was considered. Fifteen ex-27th TFW F-111Gs (including one, 68-0272, pulled from AMARC storage for RAAF service as A8-272 'The Boneyard Wrangler') were refurbished by Sacramento Air Logistics Center and delivered to the RAAF through to May 1994. The remaining F-111Gs went to AMARC, with 68-0247 the last to arrive there.

F-111K

The RAF version was essentially an F-111A with FB-111A wing extensions and undercarriage units, an extra fuselage centreline fuel tank pylon and an extending in-flight refuelling probe ahead of the windshield. The nose section

A 494th TFS F-111F (72-1443) heading out for the Bardenas Reales range to drop Mk 82 AIRs during a weapons training detachment to Zaragosa AB, Spain. The F-111's high speed at low altitude was its main defence against the hordes of Soviet fighters that the aircraft would have encountered in its original nuclear deep-strike role. At low altitude, F-111s were substantially faster than their B-1B Lancer and B-2A Spirit successors. (USAF)

had three cameras for the intended strike/reconnaissance role. Some F-111Ks were also to be configured as TF-111K strike/trainers. The weapons bay would have housed an extending ejector rack or a British-produced reconnaissance pallet similar to the RF-111A's. Two airframes, an F-111K and a TF-111K (UK serials XV884 and XV885), had been completed out of the 50 ordered when the order was cancelled in 1968, and parts of them were used for GD test purposes while the rest were diverted to FB-111A production.

OPERATIONAL HISTORY

Airborne in the Aardvark

In official language, training regimes for the F-111 required 'a complete familiarity with one's crew position, the responsibilities thereof and a working knowledge of the other crew-member's duties'. In practice that meant changed procedures and attitudes for crew members who often came from very different backgrounds. A quarter of the original 'right-seaters' came from SAC B-52s or B-58As; others were newly trained but saw the WSO's seat as an interim stage in upgrading to the pilot's position. Some had experience of the 'crew co-ordination' in two-seat F-4 Phantom IIs. Often, it worked well. Lt Col Steve Altick recalled the early F-111D days:

> My WSO, Major Stan Souska, had a SAC background and was very steady, didn't want any 'stick' [piloting] time but was fearless and trusted the pilot even on 200ft altitude TFR missions at night. The avionics were a considerable jump for everybody, especially for ex-F-100 drivers like myself. As an instructor pilot we learned how to use the radar and got pretty good at dropping bombs. The new WSOs were easy to fly with, mostly brand new and willing to learn.

For Col Joe Kittinger, MiG killer and vice-commander of the 48th TFW as it transitioned from the F-4D Phantom II, moving to the F-111F wasn't an option as he 'didn't relish the idea of becoming a bomber pilot'.

WSO Lt Col Bob Brotzman commanded the 391st TFS on F-111As but previously flew 130 F-4 Phantom II combat missions. He felt that the F-111 was more suited to the two-pilot cockpit than the F-4.

The flight controls were more fully replicated in the right seat than they had been in the F-4 'pit' [rear cockpit]. The throttles fully controlled the engines, unlike the Phantom where you couldn't get into afterburner from the back seat. You also had a good view to the front for take-off and landing, unlike the F-4, and with a little stretching you could easily reach across the left-seater to operate the landing gear. I've often reached across a napping or busy aircraft commander to adjust the wing sweep. Flight instruments were also more comprehensive in the right seat than the Phantom's pathetically limited 'pit' set.

Initially, however, the concept presented difficulties for an effective weapons system due to lack of 'right seat' expertise. Bob Brotzman recalls:

They would just take off, engage auto-TFR and proceed until the INS said to drop the weapons on the target they had inserted [on the mission cassette]. Their blind trust in the 'magic' probably resulted in aircraft losses and almost certainly in targets missed by miles. There would be the occasional right-seat pilot who had an aptitude for and an interest in learning the intricacies of the whole weapons system, but they were the exceptions.

This situation was particularly evident for the F-111D. Bob Brotzman again:

The F-111D's Mk II avionics were a nightmare for TAC for the first few years. It was truly state-of-the-art stuff, but I would say that part of the reason for the terrible teething problem was the right-seat pilots who, when confronted with problems and malfunctions in flight, were prone to turn everything off and 'go visual'. They hadn't been selected for their aptitude in systems operation, and they knew their ultimate path to success would not be through being good in the right seat.

Fortunately, Bob Brotzman was among the WSOs who were 'fascinated by this early application of digital computing to tactical flight. We were soon involved in the early software changes that slowly but surely began to make the F-111D more useable and reliable'.

Learning to fly the F-111 presented new challenges, particularly the auto-TFR, but the climate around Nellis AFB in Nevada gave little opportunity to develop all-weather skills. Lt Col Ed Wells trained many crews:

There is precious little WX [weather] in Nevada but TFR, both manual and auto were what we did essentially, and of course dropping bombs. We trained both WSOs and pilots but not together as a crew because their final assignments were undetermined. As instructor pilots we were trained in both right and left seats. I've flown [F-111Es] at low level, at night over the highlands of Scotland, and the route went directly over Loch Ness (narrow) and Loch Lomond (big and wide). One of the more interesting things about auto-TFR is that when the aircraft crests a rise, like the mountains surrounding these lochs, it pushes over into darkness and nothing. This is when your nerves are on edge before the attack radar comes in and the WSO can scan the terrain ahead to see where you are headed. As the bird levels out the radar altimeter locks onto the surface of the loch water and holds a perfect set altitude. It's still a little creepy, and I would always have my WSO remove the 'boot' on his radar-scope so that I could see what was happening as well.

In many circumstances weather was just as challenging. Lt Col Wells had to investigate the fatal crash of one of his F-111Es (68-0018 with Lt Cols Floyd Sweet and Kenneth Blank, 55th TFS commander and F-105 MiG killer) in January 1972 as it approached RAF Leuchars, Scotland.

> The crew were flying in snow showers and on a GCA [ground-controlled approach] when a low mountain appeared out of the murk. They snapped the nose up, the bird stalled and the right-seater pulled the handle to eject. They hit the ground, which interrupted the very brief millisecond ejection sequence, and 19,000lb of JP-4 fuel in the main tank directly behind the capsule exploded and shredded everything in front of the wings.

Bird-strikes were a major worry on most low-level routes. F-111E 68-0081 with Capt 'Duke' Wolf and Maj Tony Miller (WSO) aboard took a bird-strike near Shap Fell on 5 March 1975.

> They were lucky as they were at 1,000ft – in those areas birds forced us up to 1,000ft. They took a bird in the windscreen, before we got ['bird-proof'] polycarbonate windscreens, and immediately the right side panel popped out. The WSO immediately got his head caught in the airstream and thought he was going to suffocate. He couldn't breathe until he managed to force his head down below the slipstream. The vibration was so bad that the pilot couldn't control the airplane and they had to eject. We also had a bird drive the intake spike into a fuel cell in another airplane and it caught fire. The big problem we had with losing planes, though, was the bleed-air duct that put hot air into the wheel-well, causing a total system failure.

Take-off in the F-111 usually needed full afterburner, though this could cause tyre skidding with aircraft weights above 60,000lb. The rudder became effective at about 60kt, nosewheel steering was disengaged and the control stick pulled back at 15kt below take-off speed. On lift-off the pilot maintained 10 degrees of pitch attitude while the flaps and landing gear retracted before reaching 295kt. For landing, wing sweep was set to 16–20 degrees, depending on landing weight. Landing gear was extended below 295kt, and slats were deployed at around 250kt. Flaps were first lowered to 15 degrees, then fully as the F-111 slowed to around 220kt. A turn into 'finals' was made at around 160kt, descending at 600–700ft per minute. On touchdown, the engines were throttled back to idle, automatically extending the spoilers. Nose-gear steering and differential braking were engaged. Angle of attack for landing was usually 10 degrees. Below 90kt the stick could be pulled fully aft to use the stabilator for aerodynamic braking. Taxi speed was limited to 25kt (10kt on turns) to prevent brakes and tyres overheating.

F-111E 67-0120 provides reminders of its dual conventional and nuclear warfare roles, with 19 bomb scores beneath its windshield for missions flown from Incirlik AB, Turkey during Operation *Proven Force* and a practice B61 nuclear weapon (BDU-38) on its outer pylon. Real B61s were silver and were carried on the inboard pylons, with 600 US gallon external fuel tanks usually hung on the outer pylons. This jet alternated with 68-0020 as the 20th TFW commander's aircraft, 'The Chief', for a time before preservation at the IWM Museum, Duxford. (Author's collection)

F-111A operations

The distinctive *Combat Lancer* rudder emblem appears on this F-111A, which also has the two AN/ALQ-87 ECM pods required to defeat the North Vietnamese radar threats facing the Aardvarks in 1968. Initially, there was some consideration given to using Convair B-58A Hustlers for these all-weather, night-time attacks. However, *Combat Bullseye* tests had shown that the F-111A achieved better bombing scores than the B-58A. (Tom Germscheid)

F-111A 66-0018, assigned to the *Combat Lancer* commander, Col Ivan Dethman, with a thin red, white and blue stripe painted behind the cockpit. It flew the first mission of the deployment on 25 March 1968, hitting an armament dump on Tiger Island. In a 'second life' it became an EF-111A, flying with the 429th ECS until the late 1990s. (Tom Germsheid)

The first operational F-111A (66-0013, later converted into an EF-111A Raven) flew 1,047 miles from Fort Worth, Texas to Nellis AFB, Nevada at 1,000ft altitude, mainly in auto-TFR. Two aircraft flew across the Atlantic from Loring AFB, Maine to the Paris Air Show in May 1967 without in-flight refuelling. The aircraft's safety record had been acceptable: three serious accidents in the first 5,000 hours of flying was less than a third of the record of most other contemporary fighters. During the first 750,000 flight hours the F-111A became the safest of the Century Series aircraft: 73 accidents compared with 471 for the F-100 Super Sabre.

Encouraging Category II service acceptance trials by the first 18 F-111As, set against political opposition to the programme, persuaded the USAF in April 1967 to prove the aircraft in the Vietnam War combat environment. Category III service testing was brought forward and F-111As were moved to Nellis AFB for the 4481st TFS, 4480th TFW's *Harvest Reaper* programme. The aircraft were modified to carry AN/ALQ-87 jamming pods and used for the pre-deployment training programme called *Combat Trident*. This included an exercise where new pilots were told to put their hands on their helmets while the TFR flew the aircraft automatically over mountainous terrain at 200ft altitude in 'hard ride' mode. In preparation for Southeast Asia, local tree height had to be considered in planning TFR routes, as some trees grew to 200ft. Routes parallel to ridgelines and along valley floors provided the best terrain masking. Terrain features that would not require afterburner to get over them were chosen, thus reducing the chances of visual detection at night.

E During the F-111A's second deployment to Vietnam, the 474th TFW 'Roadrunners' carried out many attacks on transport targets in the months leading up to Operation *Linebacker II*. These included a river ford and bridge near Ban Karai in Southern Laos, hit by Maj Robert Mack Brown and Maj Robert D. Morrissey on the night of 7 September 1972. After dropping their bombs their F-111A (67-0063, 'Whaler 57' from the 429th TFS) disappeared, apparently hit by gunfire from the 359th Company of the Quang Binh forces. Because the F-111As generally operated alone at low altitude, losses were often unexplained. A small amount of associated debris was found 20 years later.

The 474th TFW deployed to Vietnam twice to fly all-weather, nocturnal interdiction sorties of the kind pioneered by 'Ryan's Raiders' crews flying modified F-105F Thunderchiefs. The F-111A's greater range, weapon load and radar bombing capability made it more suitable even though it had not yet completed its USAF service trials. It did not require tankers (except in emergencies), ECM support or fighter escort.

The initial Combat Lancer deployment to Takhli Royal Thai Air Force Base (RTAFB), Thailand from March to November 1968 took six early production F-111As and their crews, all with less than 100 hours on the type. In 55 otherwise successful sorties, two aircraft disappeared without trace; and a third, from which the crew escaped, suffered control loss due to a failed tailplane actuator valve, as did F-111A 66-0032 near Nellis AFB on 8 May 1968. Difficulty with TFR in heavy rainstorms, where its forward vision was blanked out, may also have been a factor. These accidents stirred the media into even more vitriolic criticism of the F-111, obscuring the overall success of the Takhli detachment in flying nocturnal missions below 500ft in very challenging climatic conditions. 'Senators Urge Recall of Suicide F-111' was one typically ill-informed headline.

The 474th TFW deployed to Takhli RTAFB again on 27 September 1972 with two complete squadrons in Constant Guard V when bombing of North Vietnam resumed. They were in combat near Hanoi 33 hours after leaving Nellis AFB and remained in Thailand until June 1975. By mid-October 1972 the F-111As had accounted for half the USAF strikes against North Vietnam; and as Maj Gen Eugene Hudson (Seventh AF Director of Intelligence) observed, 'The mere presence of 24 sorties a night striking at random and without warning throughout North Vietnam must have caused considerable consternation'. Initially, they concentrated on similar targets to those selected during Combat Lancer: storage areas, transport and suspected troop concentrations. Often, these missions were flown above cloud using radar beacon bombing, or the F-111A's radar offset bombing capability.

When Operation *Linebacker II* began on 18 December 1972, F-111As were heavily involved in supporting B-52 attacks on the Hanoi area. MiG airfields, SAM sites and other military installations were targeted in many of the 4,000 sorties flown by March 1973. The 474th TFW 'Roadrunners' battled with MiGs, SAMs and the heaviest anti-aircraft defences ever assembled. Although six F-111As were destroyed, the loss rate was 0.15 per cent, the lowest for any US combat aircraft during the war. Several MiGs attempted interceptions and many SAMs were fired, but no F-111A was a confirmed loss to either threat.

Jack Funke encountered a MiG during a mission against the Paul Doumer bridge.

WSO Capt Richard B. Tourtellot and a full load of Mk 82 low-drag general purpose (LDGP) bombs, ready for another *Constant Guard V* mission. This ordnance replaced the bomb-load of four Mk 84 2,000lb LDGPs after several of the latter armed themselves immediately after leaving their pylons at low altitude, possibly causing otherwise unexplained losses. (Lee Dodd)

We flew the 40-mile approach at 200ft clearance. Almost immediately Paul, my WSO, reported MiG-frequency radar signals at our 3 o'clock. We picked up its blue navigation lights as it converted to a tail chase. Paul could detect lock-on attempts, which he could defeat with our ECM. The guy followed us all the way to our IP [Initial Point] but couldn't get down to our level. I was worried because we had to climb to 400ft for bomb release. I delayed the climb until the last minute and popped up with 10 seconds to go, then immediately went down to 200ft after bombing. Just as we were in the descent and starting a left turn, a 37mm gun opened up. I thought we were hit as the flashes were big and we could feel five impacts – the shock waves from the passing rounds. We took no hits but we checked the hydraulic pressure about 10,000 times on the way back. Meanwhile, the MiG had trailed us in but apparently lost us when the bombs went off. I had rolled level after the 37mm scare, when suddenly I noticed the blue lights at our 10 o'clock, passing on our left and climbing out. Here was where we needed our 20mm gun! With 10 degrees nose-up and 30 degrees left we could have had a MiG kill!

Paul and I bombed the northwest rail-line near Yen Bai, several SAM sites, Phuc Yen and Kep airfields. The only time we had a SAM launch against us was the Phuc Yen mission. The SAM operators couldn't track us at 200ft, but on this occasion they guided the SAM manually. It exploded behind us and post-flight inspection revealed one tiny puncture in one of the elevons.

F-111A 67-0088 was a 429th TFS *Constant Guard V* participant that moved to the 347th TFW at Korat RTAFB for two years from June 1973, flying missions over Laos and Cambodia, many of them medium-altitude 'beacon bombing' sorties. This aircraft was transferred to the 366th TFW post-war and served until retirement in June 1991. (Author's collection)

The deployment changed perceptions of the F-111, as *Constant Guard V* veteran Capt Brad Insley observed:

> The longer we were flying sorties the more they discovered our capability. We started getting targets that only we could hit effectively, like airfields and SAM sites. The crews knew what the airplane could do and how to do it, but the planners had to be convinced.

After *Linebacker II*, the 'Roadrunners' flew missions over Laos and Cambodia. Many involved 'blind' radar offset bombing from medium altitude; or pathfinder sorties using the F-111A's superior bombing/navigation equipment to lead other aircraft to their targets. Transferred to the 347th TFW at Korat RTAFB in July 1973, the F-111As continued these missions and also participated in the recovery of the crew of the SS *Mayaguez*, captured by the Cambodian Khmer Rouge in May 1975, before returning to Nellis AFB the following month.

Digital 'Pigs'

F-111D 27th TFW

The 522nd TFS 'Fireballs' converted from F-100 Super Sabres to the F-111E in 1969, using them as trainers pending the arrival of F-111Ds from 1 November 1971. The 'Fireballs' became the first combat-ready F-111D squadron in November 1972. Lt Col Steve Altick was in at the start.

> I was one of the initial instructor pilots in the F-111D, picking them up from the factory and beginning to transition at Cannon AFB. The avionics were amazing for the time and did take some getting used to. The flat screen [display] was the first of what is a common feature of aircraft now. All of us had some confidence-building time with the TFR. I always kept a careful eye on the scope and had my own parameters for taking over the control stick. The hardest parts were the auto-TFR descents to 500ft at night. I ended up with a high level of confidence in the TFR system and the aircraft. Almost all the F-111D pilots were trained on the F-111A or F-111F first. The aircraft flew similarly but the avionics provided the learning curve.

Bob Brotzman observed that 'the F-111A/E had basically quite similar avionics to the F-4 Phantom – analogue ballistics and navigation computers with lots of rats whirring their respective treadmills', plus a more accurate INS, far superior attack radar and a TFR.

> The guts of the avionics were not much advanced from the Phantom in terms of automating the flight experience, but the F-111D was light years beyond; a truly staggering advance in capability that was not matched in tactical aviation until the F-15E Strike Eagle became operational in the 1990s. The F-111D was quite simply an aircraft that 'helped' you accomplish the mission more than any other at the time.

The 'Fireballs' made the first overseas F-111D deployment in September 1978, flying to Norway for Exercise *Northern Wedding*; and to Boscombe Down, UK for Exercise *Coronet Hammer* with 18 aircraft in 1980. Further Boscombe Down deployments included *Coronet Archer* in September 1983, *Coronet Comanche* in September 1986 (with six 390th ECS EF-111As), and *Coronet Diamond* in June 1989 with 12 F-111Ds. Bob Pahl led eight 522nd TFS F-111Ds in for the 1983 *Coronet Archer* visit:

They didn't want to use tankers so we went from Cannon to Pease AFB, then Goose Bay, Labrador, then Keflavik and Boscombe Down. At Cannon our take-off runs were 4,200ft but at Boscombe Down, which is nearly at sea level, the take-off rolls were spectacular and the airplane performed outstandingly. Unfortunately, every sortie was in support of the *Reforger* exercise [in West Germany]. Those sorties into Europe were very long and we couldn't fly at night. It would have been very useful for the crews to have experience of operating in the UK air traffic environment because all the guys were going to end up in units in the UK.

The 'Fireballs' won the Best F-111 Crew Award at the SAC Bombing and Navigation competitions in 1979 and 1980, having also participated in 1974 and 1977. Bob Brotzman recalled their first (1974) appearance, initially viewed somewhat sardonically by the 27th TFW:

No real bombs, no TFR, no proper speed – it ain't worth the effort! We didn't think the SAC Radar Bomb Scoring sites scored very accurately so we did much of our initial work-up on the Green River Utah Bomb-plot with more sophisticated radars. The approach to the target took one through the rugged canyon lands of Utah and so we loved to scream along below the lip of the canyons, flipping the big 'Vark one way then the other before popping up at 10 miles from the target and announcing the beginning of our bomb run. It was completely against the spirit and intent of the boring SAC competition! Exercise *Giant Voice* was flown over two nights and the sorties were very long for TAC crews. There was a medium-altitude bomb run, then you descended lower (but not 'properly' low) for a Large Charge (two bomb runs in immediate succession), then you climbed out and did it all again an hour later.

F-111Ds of the 522nd TFS 'Fireballs' from Cannon AFB over Egypt during the 1983 Exercise *Bright Star* deployment to Cairo West AB. Deriving from the Camp David Accords, these biennial combined forces, multi-national demonstrations of ongoing support for Egypt began in 1980 and continued after Operation *Desert Storm.* (USAF)

When we landed after Sortie 1 we were in second place out of about 20 crews! As we climbed out of the last bomb run we felt an impact on the airframe. Fred Zehr [pilot] had flown in Vietnam in F-105s and I was in Phantoms and we both said the same thing: 'We've taken a hit!' The jet seemed to be flying OK, all indications were normal, so we pressed on to recover at Barksdale AFB. Across the fence at about 210kt we needed most of Barksdale's runway to get stopped. People started pointing and making faces as we left the runway and it soon became obvious that we'd had a collision with a large bird which had hit us directly in the left slat, creating a large hole into the structure of the wing [of F-111D 68-0164].

Cannon-based F-111Ds also deployed to South Korea (*Team Spirit*) from 1981, Egypt (*Bright Star*) in 1983, Elmendorf, Alaska (*Brim Frost*) and *Maple Flag*, Canada in 1992. Bob Pahl led a three-week *Team Spirit* deployment via Hickam AFB, Hawaii with tankers. 'We flew day and night low-level sorties into the DMZ [De-Militarized Zone] between North and South Korea, including some flying up into the areas of bad weather.' F-111Ds were replaced by ex-48th TFW F-111Fs from February 1992 and the Vietnam-veteran 428th FS 'Buccaneers' then became the training squadron, with a six-month course of 35 flights for new undergraduates. From 1990 it had F-111Gs, succeeded by F-111Es in 1992. Foreign deployments to Korea and Panama and Australia were made by Cannon's 523rd TFS 'Crusaders' (redesignated as the 523rd FS from October 1991) after transitioning to the F-111D in 1973. Cannon AFB became the last home to all the F-111s remaining in the USAF inventory, including ex-USAFE F-111E/Fs.

Strategic Swingers

FB-111A
The first of 14 FB-111As (airframes 8 to 22) to be delivered to the 340th BG was 67-0193, flown in to Carswell AFB, Texas on 29 September 1969 by Col Winston Moore, the commander of the 4007th CCTS, 340th BG, to begin 20 years of FB-111A service life. Many FB-111A crews came from the B-58A Hustler or from B-52 Stratofortresses. Selection required 2,000 hours for pilots and 1,500 hours for WSOs. After delivery of seven FB-111As, problems arose with their TFR and wing longeron structure, leading to a mandatory 'Recovery Program' in late 1969. Testing and structural inspection continued until July 1971. The final (15th) aircraft for the 4007th CCTS was received in May 1971. The other FB-111A wings were the 380th BW at Plattsburgh AFB, New York, which received its first aircraft in July 1971, and the 509th BW (Medium) at Pease AFB, New Hampshire, from December 1970. The 4007th CCTS moved its training activities to Plattsburgh AFB in December 1971 and became the 530th CCTS in July 1986.

FB-111A bases were located in New England to allow for the FB-111A's shorter range to Soviet targets compared with that of the B-52, although Cold War interdiction missions would still have terminated in Turkey or Iceland. SAC had 72 FB-111As on charge in 1974 and 66 in 1977, rotating the $9.8m aircraft to satellite alert airfields like McGuire AFB, New Jersey and Kincheloe AFB, Michigan in the early 1970s. During SAC reorganization in March 1970, the Eighth Air Force was redistributed between the Second and Fifteenth air forces and the Second Air Force took over the FB-111A wings.

The first FB-111A participation in a SAC bombing and navigation competition was in 1970, with two 340th BW aircraft participating alongside

28 B-52s, 28 KC-135s and four RAF Vulcans. The 340th BW aircraft won the wing bombing trophy and narrowly missed the navigation award. The 380th BW(M) took top honours for five years between 1974 and 1984 and the 509th BW won the top awards each year from 1979 to 1983. In 1989 FB-111A and F-111D participants took all three places for the Curtis Le May Trophy.

Many FB-111A sorties were flown over the Nellis AFB *Red Flag* ranges for training at altitudes as low as 100ft at over 600kt. Operation *Tea Party* was the 19 July 1986 deployment of five 509th BW FB-111As to RAF Mildenhall for a NATO exercise, this being the first FB-111A deployment to the UK. The FB-111A became extremely reliable during the 1980s as problems were ironed out, particularly after the AMP updates.

The AGM-69A SRAM was withdrawn in June 1990 due to propellant in the missiles becoming unstable through age and concerns about its nuclear warhead in the event of an aircraft fire. This effectively ended the FB-111A's alert role. The first ex-509th BW FB-111A, having been converted to an F-111G and reassigned to the 27th TFW, was flown to Cannon AFB by Maj Gen Charles Searock Jr and Lt Col George Kramlinger on 1 June 1990 for F-111D/F training with the 428th TFTS. The last two left Pease AFB on 5 September 1990 and the 509th BW's 393rd BS prepared for conversion to the B-2A Spirit. The F-111Gs were initially scheduled to be based in the UK as a third USAF wing, but were actually replaced at Cannon AFB by formerly UK-based AMP F-111Es by mid-July 1993.

An ordnance crew practises loading B61 nuclear weapons into the weapons bay of an FB-111A. Later versions of this weapon could deploy a 24ft diameter parachute, allowing supersonic delivery at altitudes down to 50ft. It was manufactured from 1966 to 1987 and 3,150 were produced. (USAF)

USAFE

F-111E
The first two F-111Es for the 20th TFW (68-0035 and -0045) arrived at RAF Upper Heyford on 12 September 1970, led in by 20th TFW commander Col Grant A. Smith. Lt Col Edwin Wells was among the first group of F-111E pilots at Upper Heyford in 1970.

> The 79th TFS was the first to switch to the 'Vark [by January 1971] and the 77th TFS was second. The 55th TFS [in which Wells was a flight commander] continued to fly F-100D/Fs until the spring of 1971. Many of the 'Hun' [F-100] jocks rotated to new assignments, but anyone who had sufficient time remaining on their tour went to Nellis for academics and flight training in the 'big beast'.

Col Ron Barker was also a 55th TFS flight commander as the squadron transitioned to the F-111E.

> We didn't have any of the old 'Hun' drivers from the 55th. We got our brand-new F-111Es, one or two at a time, and the crews came in slow but steady. We had WSOs paired up with every pilot. Every pilot outranked his WSO.

'Land Shark' (F-111E 68-062), in full 79th TFS 'Tigers' squadron colours and hauling an AN/ALQ-131 ECM pod under its rear fuselage in 1988. Applying to use the nickname, its crew chief wrote: 'While at Red Flag, when flying low-level over the desert the only visible sign of the F-111 was the vertical stabilizer. The "enemy" (Aggressor fighter pilots) nicknamed the F-111 a "Land Shark"'. (Author)

Ed Wells recalled:

> They extended everyone's tours from three to four years, which meant we were 'locked in'! We had some of the best low-level routes anywhere, from France to the tip of Scotland, and we used several radar bombing sites as well as live drops on Jurby range (off the Isle of Man) and Wainfleet in the Wash for day or night low-altitude bombing.

Bob Pahl explained:

> The F-4 Phantoms IIs didn't have the 'legs' that we had, so they got priority on Wainfleet and Holbeach [day-only ranges], and Jurby became one of our primary ranges. All we did was level [bombing] patterns there. We had standard linked routes and a range block-booked. As low-level routes got canned and you didn't have to draw them up each time, you'd just pull one off the shelf.
>
> At Upper Heyford we had an A, B or C launch schedule with about two hours for each squadron. There were two morning squadrons (that lingered into the late afternoon) and the night squadron. We didn't inter-mingle the squadrons. Each sortie had two hours planning time plus mission preparation time. For 'sortie surge' exercises you might fly two missions back-to-back. Over Germany, we were very limited as to where we could fly and there were many noise restrictions, and we were limited to 750ft minimum altitude. The German Air Force used to fly under us! In the UK it was 500ft minimum and 1,000ft at night. I was surprised when I got to Mountain Home where they flew at 200ft at night. It wasn't until the 1980s that we were allowed to fly in bad weather in the UK, and then only in selected areas.

At Upper Heyford, nine aircraft were kept on 15-minute Victor alert with nuclear weapons. NATO's two wings of F-111s, based in the UK, faced overwhelmingly larger Soviet Bloc forces, but their speciality was airfield attack and interdiction to cut logistical supply lines to advancing enemy forces. Their ability to fly at low altitude in radar 'ground clutter' offered the best protection against the numerous hostile interceptors and compensated for their comparatively small numbers. It was their success in weather conditions that grounded other NATO aircraft during exercises like *Cold Fire* and *Central Enterprise* that persuaded the USAF to base more F-111s in Europe, leading to the transfer of F-111Fs to the UK.

Originally, the F-111Ds of the 27th TFW were due to replace F-4Ds at RAF Lakenheath, UK in the air-to-air and air-to-ground roles. 'The F-111D', as Col Bob Pahl recalled, 'had so many problems that they kept it at Cannon. The avionics proved to be very difficult to work on and they didn't have adequate funding.' Later, contingency plans existed to deploy additional F-111Ds from Cannon AFB and, like the F-111E and F-111F, they would have been able to

Final checks for 'Remit 31' (F-111F 70-2390 of the 495th TFS) as it prepares to take off for the longest fighter mission in history on 14 April 1986. Its four GBU-10C/B bombs hit Colonel Gaddafi's headquarters complex in Tripoli later that night as part of Operation *El Dorado Canyon*. During the outbound flight, 'Remit 31's crew were still studying photocopies of the detailed mission information that had been handed to them (after many revisions) just before they prepared to take off. (USAF)

fly to about a third of the pre-planned NATO targets with around 6,000lb of bombs. Ordnance, as Bob Pahl recalled, was

> strictly dumb bombs, with no LGBs, not even buddy-lasing. When I was at Cannon AFB we practised buddy-lasing extensively with the F-111D day and night, mainly with RF-4Cs with laser capability (PAVE Tack). You really had to synchronize your manoeuvre with the RF-4C. It was better if we had a guy on the ground who could lase the target.

The 42nd ECS 'NATO Ravens' was recommissioned on 1 July 1983 and joined the 20th TFW, although its parent unit became the 66th ECW at Sembach, West Germany in June 1985. The first of 13 EF-111As for the squadron (66-037, 'NATO Raven One') was delivered on 3 February 1984, piloted by Lt Col David Vesely and Maj Roger Brooks. The Ravens displayed colourful nose-art in 1987, initiated by Capt Kent Malcom RCAF (Royal Canadian Air Force), who was running 42nd AMU. The aircraft played important roles in Operation *El Dorado Canyon* in 1986 and deployed to Incirlik AB in Turkey and both Al Kharj AB and Dhahran AB in Saudi Arabia for operations *Desert Storm* and *Provide Comfort*. In June 1992 the squadron began to transfer its aircraft to the 390th ECS 'Ravens' at Mountain Home AFB prior to deactivation of the 42nd ECS on 10 July 1992.

F-111F

Squadron service began with the 347th TFW at Mountain Home AFB, Idaho on 20 September 1971 and the wing's three squadrons, the 389th TFS 'Thunderbolts', 390th TFS 'Boars' and 391st TFS 'Bold Tigers', became operational in October 1972. Training concentrated on low-altitude, night TFR sorties. Two deployments were made to South Korea in 1976 in response to increased tensions with North Korea. The aircraft were transferred to the 48th TFW's 492nd, 493rd, 494th (first to re-equip) and 495th TFS (the last being the 'Aardvark University' training squadron) at RAF Lakenheath in the complex Project *Creek Swing/Ready Switch* from 1 June 1977.

In this rare image, one of the 'Karma' cell of F-111Fs approaches its tanker to refuel as night falls. 'Karma' cell was the last of three cells to hit Gaddafi's centre of power during Operation *El Dorado Canyon*, and it sustained the only loss of the complex mission when 'Karma 52' (70-2389) hit the sea short of the Tripoli coastline with the loss of Maj Fernando Ribas Dominici and WSO Capt Paul Lorence. It is possible that they were hand-flying their aircraft at less than 100ft altitude and over 600kt after their TFR radar was jammed by interference from Libyan SAM radars. (via Jim Rotramel)

For Bob Pahl, the F-111F was 'the perfect F-111'; and Col Dave Reiner, commander of two 366th TFW squadrons, regarded it as 'the Cadillac of the fleet'. Although it was similar to previous F-111s, from the pilot's viewpoint it required extensive retraining for right-seaters moving from the analogue systems of previous models to the F-111F's digital avionics, which in Lt Col Bill Baker's opinion gave a 'leap in capability', with a second leap provided by the PAVE Tack targeting pod after January 1981. Pilots welcomed the extra power of the TF30-P-100 engines and the fact that the TFR allowed low-altitude turns at 30-degree bank angles rather than the 10-degree limit of the F-111A.

Training regimes were similar to those at RAF Upper Heyford, including weapons training detachments (WTDs) to Zaragoza AB, Spain and Incirlik AB, Turkey, with occasional appearances at *Red Flag* and *Green Flag* exercises on the Nellis AFB ranges in Nevada. The wing became specialists with new weaponry like the Paveway III LGB and the GBU-15 glide-bomb (a 493rd TFS speciality), and in *Desert Storm* the 4,700lb GBU-28/B 'bunker-buster' bomb. After its outstanding combat operations over Libya and Iraq, the 48th TFW began to transition to the F-15E Strike Eagle. The first F-111F to leave RAF Lakenheath was 70-2386 (the 'high-time' F-111, with 6,277.7 flight hours) on 10 August 1991, and the 494th TFS 'Panthers' ended RAF Lakenheath's F-111F era in July 1992. Many crews transferred to the 27th TFW with their F-111Fs.

One Night in Libya

The 48th TFW was chosen for a punitive USAFE strike, Operation *El Dorado Canyon*, against Libyan military facilities after seven years of terrorist activities against US and European civilians instigated by the country's leader, Colonel Gaddafi. Contingency planning at RAF Lakenheath began on 1 January 1986 and envisaged a strike with LGBs by four or six F-111Fs. Practice runs for the longest fighter mission in history (and the first for the USAF since Vietnam) were flown by the 20th TFW across the Atlantic and 27th TFW within the USA. By 7 April 1986 the mission had expanded to include a much larger strike force acting in unison with strikes from US Navy aircraft carriers in the Mediterranean. France, Spain and Italy refused overflights by the 'armada' of 24 F-111Fs (including six air-spares), four EF-111As, and a fleet of 29 KC-10A Extenders and KC-135A Stratotankers from which the F-111s would refuel five times. This restriction added 2,600 miles and seven hours to the journey on an extended route over the Bay of Biscay and through the Gibraltar Straits. F-111F crews spent around 14 hours in the cockpit, in radio silence and mainly in darkness.

'Miss Liberty II' was assigned to 48th TFW commander, Col Tom Lennon, and is seen here marked with 29 bomb scores, hardened aircraft shelter and tank kills, as well as the colours of the 494th AMU that looked after it. (via Jim Rotramel)

The big formations for Operation *El Dorado Canyon* took off from Lakenheath, Mildenhall, Fairford and Upper Heyford at sunset on 14 April, heading out over the southwest coast without attracting undue attention despite acute media curiosity. Three EF-111As, 'hand-flown' at 200ft with their TFRs switched off to avoid detection, led the F-111Fs in to the Libyan coast and then set up offshore jamming orbits there. Three groups of F-111Fs at very low altitude made virtually simultaneous TFR-guided attacks on three targets in the Tripoli area, while US Navy strike aircraft bombed targets to the east around Benghazi. Two cells of F-111Fs hit Tripoli Airport's military area, though two aircraft had to abandon their attacks after technical problems and only the first F-111F on target achieved appreciable destruction of Libyan aircraft with its 12 Mk 82 AIR bombs.

Three cells of F-111Fs were directed at Gaddafi's power-base in the Al Azziziyah compound. Two of the aircraft directed their GBU-10E/B LGBs successfully at barracks and headquarters areas in the compound, but six abandoned their attacks because of problems with their TFRs or other systems. Rules of engagement required that the aircraft should have all their bombing/navigation systems working well before delivering ordnance to minimize collateral damage. After such an unprecedentedly long flight, with some inaccurately mapped radar offset waypoints en route, there were inevitable technical faults; but the size of the 'armada' had allowed for that.

One of the EF-111A crewmembers reported that:

All the jamming systems performed as advertised. Several times we saw missiles launched our way, but they all fell short and we never had to take evasive action. Tripoli was all lit up as the first bombs fell and thereafter the sky looked just like when Baghdad was struck during *Desert Storm*. Anyone who had a gun or missile was shooting and tracers were everywhere.

From the cockpit of F-111F 'Remit 33' in the first cell:

The target was a spectacle of sound and light. First were the Crotales [French SAMs], which skimmed the sea surface emitting a shower of sparks. The AAA (anti-aircraft artillery) included 20mm ZSU 'hoses', 50–60mm 'pom-poms' and intermittent explosions from a large-calibre gun.

The addition of a third Al Azziziyah cell was made against the Lakenheath planners' advice, and it exposed the last three aircraft to increased risk from the massive Libyan defences as the aircraft made their attack runs, separated by 30 seconds but on roughly the same tracks. One F-111F (70-2389) in that cell was lost with its crew in uncertain circumstances just offshore. Another aircraft lost sight of its target and its bombs damaged civilian buildings some distance away, including the French embassy.

The third element of the attack focused on the Sidi Bilal terrorist training camp, where three F-111Fs destroyed a training pool and small boats with GBU-10E/Bs. The formation then reassembled, located its tankers and began the exhausting journey home. One F-111F diverted to Rota NAS in Spain with a leaking hot-air pipe in its wheel-well, resulting in much international media interest. Although the attacks had inflicted less damage than the planners had hoped, the operation succeeded in its main objective. The Libyan dictator had received a clear message about the limits of American patience in tolerating terrorist activity. Thereafter, his policies eventually became more conciliatory.

Storm and Force

The 48th TFW's choice of weapons was expanded by 1991 with more accurate Paveway III LGBs, BLU-109 LGB warheads designed to penetrate hardened structures, and GBU-15 electro-optical glide-bombs. When Iraq invaded Kuwait on 2 August 1990, Operation *Desert Shield* was initiated to prevent Saddam Hussein's forces from entering Saudi Arabia as well. The 48th TFW was an obvious choice to provide long-range night interdiction and it began deploying F-111Fs on 25 August. By mid-January 1991, 67 F-111Fs were at Taif AB, Saudi Arabia, supported by 18 EF-111As from RAF Upper Heyford and Mountain Home AB as the 48th TFW (Provisional).

By 17 January, the American-led coalition forces had tired of Iraq's refusal to return to its own borders and Operation *Desert Storm* broke over military targets throughout Iraq. F-111Fs were primary elements in a massive onslaught involving cruise missiles, tactical fighter-bombers and support aircraft. The leading F-111F was 'Miss Liberty II' (70-2390), which, as 'Remit 31', had dropped the first bombs on Gaddafi's Tripoli headquarters in April 1986. Numerous Iraqi Air Force bases were main targets, and many supposedly bombproof hardened aircraft shelters and their contents were eliminated by GBU-24A/B LGBs, dropped with extreme precision using PAVE Tack lasing. Other Aardvarks used cluster bombs and GBU-24A/Bs to render the runways unusable, and GBU-10 LGBs were used against Saddam's extravagant Summer Palace at Tikrit. All F-111Fs and the vital EF-111A jammers evaded a torrent of AAA, SAMs and attempted interceptions by MiG-29s and Mirage F.1EQs, returning with superficial small-arms damage to a few aircraft.

A second Aardvark force joined the assault on 18 January, when 18 20th TFW F-111Es, with jamming provided by 42nd ECS EF-111As, all of them operating from the overcrowded Incirlik AB in Turkey, hit air-defence radar sites in northern Iraq with Mk 82 AIR bombs, following up with an attack on the Kirkuk nuclear research facility the next night. Another very heavily defended nuclear research centre at Tuwaitha was knocked out by a 48th TFW(P) crew. Among the 100 daily Operation *Proven Force* missions flown by the parent 7440th Wing (Provisional) aircraft from Incirlik AB were attacks on hydroelectric stations providing power for Mosul and military installations in Baghdad. F-111E pilot Capt Greg Stevens commented on the defences:

> I was basically picking dark spots to fly through. Everything else was lit up. Every night we said, 'When are they going to run out of bullets?'

55th TFS commander Col Simpson observed that there were

> A few SA-7 SAMs launched at our first strike but they went well behind us. The F-4G 'Wild Weasels' smacked a bunch of them and made them reluctant, but there was plenty of AAA. It was an amazing experience that I don't want to repeat.

With Iraq's air defences effectively demolished on the first night, the 48th TFW(P)'s attention turned to transport and communications, particularly Iraq's principal bridges. Joined by F-117A Nighthawks, they systematically destroyed more than 55 bridge structures with GBU-15s and GBU-24s. One of the wing's most publicized missions was flown on 26/27 January, when GBU-15s were directed from an F-111F against Kuwait's Al Ahmadi oil terminal after Iraqi forces had released millions of gallons of oil into the sea, causing an enormous slick. The GBU-15s neutralized oil-pumping facilities, stopping the leakage.

Similar ingenuity was displayed from 5 February onwards, when F-111F crews devised ways of using PAVE Tack to identify the infrared signatures of Iraqi tanks that were dug into desert revetments to protect them from conventional bombing. At night their heat signatures contrasted with the surrounding terrain sufficiently for 500lb GBU-12 LGBs to be dropped directly on to them. The first two crews to perform 'tank plinking' destroyed seven tanks with eight bombs. By 14 February the tactic was well established, and 132 armoured vehicles were destroyed in one night.

Another unique mission occurred in the closing stages of the conflict when two F-111Fs dropped newly devised 4,700lb GBU-28/B 'bunker-buster' bombs on deeply buried command bunkers beneath Al Taji airfield. The destruction wrought by one of these weapons on Saddam's senior military staff on 27 February hastened the signing of a ceasefire hours later. At Incirlik AB the 20th TFW was preparing to use a newly arrived AMP-modified F-111E to 'pathfind' for other F-111Es, using its superior high-altitude bombing accuracy to guide their ordnance drops. Another plan called for PAVE Tack-equipped F-4E Phantom IIs to 'buddy lase' LGBs for the F-111Es. Both projects were curtailed by the ceasefire, but some Aardvarks and Ravens remained in the area for Operation *Provide Comfort* (the protection of the Kurdish population of Northern Iraq).

Australian Aardvarks

Twenty-four F-111Cs were delivered in Project *Peace Lamb* from June to December 1973. Two squadrons, Nos 1 and 6 of No 82 Wing, flew the F-111 at RAAF Amberley near Brisbane, using a number of 'bare base' forward locations also. One of these, Tindal in the Northern Territory, was used to support UN activity during a period of unrest in East Timor in 1999, when Indonesia threatened to shoot down any F-111s overflying the area. When Indonesian forces finally withdrew in October 1999, RF-111C reconnaissance flights over East Timor began the only operational use of RAAF Aardvarks. F-111Cs deployed to USAF *Red Flag* exercises several times and visited the UK. Maritime strike was practiced on Australian and New Zealand naval vessels in Longex 'coastal defence' exercises using two-aircraft attacks. The defence of 'island Australia's' extensive coast from attack by sea was a major priority. Adding the AIM-9B (later AIM-9M) Sidewinder AAM provided a long-range air defence element beyond the reach of the RAAF's F/A-18A Hornets.

Lt Col William Baker, USAF, flew an exchange tour with No 6 Squadron from 1976.

> The RAAF generated different low-level routes over all terrain without FAA [Federal Aviation Administration] limitations, ensuring that they could perform in all flight conditions over land and water. They regularly flew in support of Lockheed P-3 anti-submarine operations as well as co-ordinated air/naval operations throughout the Pacific region. They developed new tactics while the USAF management awaited the next war to develop new strategy and tactics.

The four RF-111Cs were operated by No 1 Squadron and they proved to be very effective long-range reconnaissance vehicles for all-weather, day and night missions, scoring well in three Reconnaissance Air Meets at Bergstrom AFB, Texas. Four ex-366th TFW F-111As (67-0109, -0112, -0113 and -0114) were bought in 1982 at 1963 prices for No 6 Sqn as attrition replacements for the four RAAF losses and to even out the fleet's flight hours. A8-109, a *Constant Guard* veteran, flew in a 2002 *Red Flag* in which the RAAF F-111Cs scored 100 per cent serviceability, and it took part in the retirement ceremony flypast in December 2010 as the world's last operational F-111. Like the other three F-111As, it had received F-111C-type wings and undercarriage and was

Condensation steams from this No 1 Sqn F-111C as it pulls hard over the Cunningham's Gap near Brisbane with LGBs and a Harpoon anti-ship missile. The success of LGBs during Operation *Desert Storm* 'tank plinking' sorties encouraged the RAAF to mount GBU-12s on BRU-3A/As, three on each outboard pylon. (RAAF)

regarded as a standard F-111C thereafter. Life extension until at least 2020, as originally intended in the Defence White Paper of 2000, would have been possible using spare ex-USAF wings to replace airframe areas with known fatigue problems. A cold-proof load test facility was built at RAAF Amberley after the Sacramento Air Logistics Center facility in California was closed down.

Retirement of the F-111 met strong opposition as there was no clear replacement for its unique long-range strike capability, but the cost-effectiveness of the RAAF's new though shorter-ranging F/A-18F Super Hornets was unarguable. There were also concerns about health problems associated with the chemicals used in the desealing and resealing process, whereby the rubber lining of the aircraft's internal fuel tanks had to be periodically removed and replaced by operators entering the tanks and using water lances to cut away the lining material. The Aardvark, or 'Pig' in Australian parlance, served the RAAF for 37 years, and the retirement flypast was led by No 6 Sqn commander Wing Cdr Michael Gray in A8-125, the first F-111C to be delivered in June 1973. Australia's Aardvarks had survived various shifts in national defence policy, moving from a principally strategic weapon to a versatile maritime strike, army support, air control and reconnaissance aircraft. For the RAAF, the 'ugly duckling' became a 'supersonic swan', though it met an ignominious end when 23 retired examples were buried at the Swanbank landfill site in November 2011. Australia rejected an offer to buy part of the USAF EF-111A fleet when it was retired.

CONCLUSION

The last F-111s left the production line in 1976, soon after the Aardvark had proved itself in Vietnam but long before its most important achievements as a Cold War interdictor and in combat over Libya and Iraq. The difficulty in finding a suitable successor initially became clear in 1978, when a USAF Tactical All-Weather Requirements Study group recommended reopening F-111 production rather than buying the F-15E Strike Eagle. Ironically, the long-term replacement was to have been another adaptation of a US Navy design, the A-12 Avenger II, cancelled in 1992 and re-born as the Joint Strike Fighter/F-35 after many years of costly project studies. A shortage of F-111s during this period of indecision actually led to 13 aircraft being expensively rebuilt rather than written off. Many more were scheduled for AMP or Pacer Strike updates, with the aim of keeping them operational until at least 2015. However, draconian defence cuts under President Bill Clinton and the political need to support newer technologies ruled this out. In Australia the rising costs of maintenance, including 'cold proof' testing, were among the arguments used to advance F-111C retirement by ten years. The RAAF had planned to absorb more recycled USAF examples and reduce flying hours in order to meet the original 2020 retirement date.

For the USAF, the allocation of each TAC F-111 variant to a single wing increased costs, as each required its own specialized support, supplies, training and maintenance. This applied particularly to the F-111D; but the expenditure was minimal compared with the cost of introducing new types, particularly the long-delayed Lockheed F-35 Lightning II. Behind all the decisions on the Aardvark's future lay the long legacy of misunderstanding concerning its purpose and qualities, dating back to its origins in the early 1960s. Paradoxically, two of Secretary of Defense Robert McNamara's other 'common' projects, the A-7 Corsair II and F-4 Phantom II, were both highly successful in USAF service from the outset, even though they too were derived from naval specifications. Clearly, the process was not so easy when most of the original design parameters were USAF-generated rather than naval. However, commonality worked for the F-111 in that a basic airframe, with variants characterized mainly by different avionics, could be adapted to different roles without prohibitively costly structural alterations.

The F-111 overcame unrealistic design goals, muddled management, inter-service conflict and ill-informed press criticism to become one of the most successful combat aircraft of the 20th century and the progenitor of an international generation of 'swing-wing' designs. Flying at low, terrain-hugging altitude, carrying half its own weight in bombs at greater speeds than its successors, the B-1B Lancer and B-2A Spirit, and giving a much smoother ride than the fixed-wing F-15E Strike Eagle that partly replaced it, the wily 'earth-pig' was in a class of its own. While it lacked the secondary air-to-air capability of the F-15E, it could carry a 6,000lb warload over 1,000 miles, significantly further than the Strike Eagle. Its demise has left a gap in tactical strike capability that has not yet been filled.

F-111C A8-144 makes the F-111's final appearance at *Red Flag* over Nevada in 2009, flying interdiction missions for the 'Blue' forces. Low-visibility No 6 Sqn markings and an FS 36118 Gunship Gray colour scheme replaced the original 'Vietnam' camouflage when the RAAF introduced ex-USAF F-111Gs in a similar scheme. (Emery/USAF)

FURTHER READING

Books

Art, Robert L., *The TFX Decision, McNamara and the Military* (Little, Brown and Co., 1968)

Clodfelter, Mark, *The Limits of Air Power* (Simon and Schuster, 1989)

Coulam, Robert F., *Illusions of Choice. The F-111 and Problems of Weapons Acquisition Reform* (Princeton University Press, 1977)

Davies, Peter E., *USAF F/EF-111 Units in Combat* (Osprey Combat Aircraft, 2014)

Davies, Peter E. and Thornborough, Anthony M., *F-111 Aardvark* (Crowood Press, 1997)

Drendel, Lou, *F-111 in Action* (Squadron/Signal, 1978)

Feldmann, Hartmut and Wills, Kevin, *USAFE Aardvarks* (AirDOC, 2006)

Gunston, Bill, *F-111* (Salamander Modern Fighting Aircraft, 1983)

Gunston, Bill, *General Dynamics F-111* (Ian Allan, 1978)

Halbersadt, Hans, *F-111 Aardvark*, Wings 4 (Windrow and Green, 1992)

Kinzey, Bert, *F-111 Aardvark in Detail and Scale* (TAB Books, 1989)

Logan, Don, *F-111 Aardvark* (Schiffer Military History, 1998)

Mann, Col. Edward C., *Thunder and Lightning* – Desert Storm *and the Airpower Debates* (Air University Press, 1995)

Lax, Mark, *From Controversy to Cutting Edge, The F-111 in Australian Service* (Commonwealth of Australia, 2010)

Miller, Jay, *General Dynamics F-111* (Aero Publishers, Inc., 1981)

Peeters, Willy, *F-111E/F Aardvark – Lock On No. 5* (Verlinden Publications, 1989)

Reynolds, Col. Richard T., *Heart of the Storm. The Genesis of the Air Campaign against Iraq* (Air University Press, 1995)

Stanik, Joseph T., *El Dorado Canyon* (Naval Institute Press, 2003)

Stevens, Rick, 'The Earth Pig', *World Air Power Journal*, Vol. 14 (Aerospace Publishing, 1993)

Thomason, Tommy, *Grumman Navy F-111B* (Naval Fighters Number 41, 1998)

Thompson, Wayne, *To Hanoi and Back. The United States Air Force and North Vietnam 1966-73* (University Press of the Pacific, 2005)

Thornborough, Anthony M., *F-111 Aardvark* (Osprey, 1993)

Thornborough, Anthony M. and Davies, Peter E., *F-111, Success in Action* (Arms and Armour Press, 1989)

Venkus, Col. Robert E., *Raid on Qaddafi* (St Martin's Press, 1992)